THOUGHT$_2$TALK

Other books from Automatic Press ♦ $\frac{V}{I}$P

Formal Philosophy
edited by Vincent F. Hendricks & John Symons
November 2005

Masses of Formal Philosophy
edited by Vincent F. Hendricks & John Symons
October 2006

Political Questions: 5 Questions for Political Philosophers
edited by Morten Ebbe Juul Nielsen
December 2006

Philosophy of Technology: 5 Questions
edited by Jan-Kyrre Berg Olsen & Evan Selinger
January 2007

Game Theory: 5 Questions
edited by Vincent F. Hendricks & Pelle Guldborg Hansen
March 2007

Philosophy of Mathematics: 5 Questions
edited by Vincent F. Hendricks & Hannes Leitgeb
June 2007

Normative Ethics: 5 Questions
edited by Jesper Ryberg & Thomas S. Petersen
June 2007

Legal Philosophy: 5 Questions
edited by Ian Farrell and Morten Ebbe Juul Nielsen
August 2007

THOUGHT$_2$TALK

A Crash Course in Reflection and Expression

Vincent F. Hendricks

Automatic Press ♦ $\frac{V}{I}$P

Automatic Press ♦ $\frac{V}{I}$P

© Vincent F. Hendricks 2006

This publication is in copyright. Subject to statuary exception and to the provisions of relevant collective licensing agreements, no reproduction of any part may take place without the written permission of the publisher.

First published 2006

Printed in the United States of America and the United Kingdom

ISBN-10   87-991013-7-8   paperback

The publisher has no responsibilities for the persistence or accuracy of URLs for external or third party Internet Web sites referred to in this publication and does not guarantee that any content on such Web sites is, or will remain, accurate or appropriate.

Typeset in $\LaTeX 2_\varepsilon$
Jacket design by Vincent F. Hendricks & Henriette Kibsgaard

For Mommy in the City,
Mimi Vang Olsen

Contents

Preface   iii

Signs and Symbols   v

1 Statements   1
    1.1 Contradictory Statements 2
    1.2 Tautological Statements 5
    1.3 Contingent Statements 6
    1.4 Nasty Statements 9

2 Arguments   11
    2.1 Argument Schemata 12
    2.2 Syntax and Semantics 18
    2.3 Back to Statements 23

3 Validities   25
    3.1 Strip to Discover 25
    3.2 Truth-Tables to Check 27
    3.3 Connectives, Paths and Trees 32
    3.4 Semantic Tableaux 35
    3.5 Checking Trees 37

4 Fallacies   41
    4.1 Jump 41
    4.2 Brute Force 43
    4.3 The Man 44
    4.4 Authority 46
    4.5 The Masses 46
    4.6 Ignorance 47
    4.7 Begging it 47
    4.8 Claim, Data and Warrant 48

5 Modalities   49
    5.1 Intensions 49
    5.2 Counterfactuals 52
    5.3 Attitudes 54

	5.4	Opinions	58
6	**Demonstrations**		**59**
	6.1	Proofs	59
	6.2	A Knowledge Primer	62
	6.3	Squaring the Opposition	72
	6.4	I Think I'm Talking	76

Further Reading   **77**

About the Author   **79**

Index   **83**

Preface

Thought₂Talk is a *crash course* on argument, reasoning, analysis and logical method honoring the Swedish poet and Bishop of Lund, Esaias Tegnér, who once said:

> The words and thoughts of men are born together: To speak obscurely is to think obscurely.[1]

Argument, reason and method are far from exhausted by this text – there is much more to it – if for no other reason because logic surrounds us every day. Used and abused at cocktail parties and dinner functions, in friendly conversations and verbal feuds, in thinking and reflecting, in any science, logic is a tool of mind. It is the language of thought. In leisure as well as business, man wants to be snap, witty and logically correct. And so, logic is part of the human condition, and concerns us all even if it is not always used by man. Considered familiar and natural when understood as synonymous with 'common-sense', 'sure', 'of course', and 'that's obvious', logic is at the same time considered alien – perhaps even boring and dry – when used in science. Logic then transforms into strange symbols, complicated formulae, Greek letters, technical illustrations, algebras and numbers, propositions, lemmata and theorems ... things out of a math-book rather than your thoughts. Logic doesn't care about labels like alien. It is about the structure of language rather than its content, and the ways we reason rather than what we reason about. Largely omitting the symbols, Greek letters and algebras one may still look at the connection between thoughts and words.

Logic is a truly interdisciplinary field. Whether you decide to go into literature, social science, computer science, history, human resources, business administration or advertising for your advanced

---

[1] Most of the quotes in this book are taken from the trilogy of humorous and critical quotations on philosophy, logic and their broader intellectual environment: *Feisty Fragments: For Philosophy* (London: King's College Publications, 2004), *Logical Lyrics: From Philosophy to Poetics* (London: King's College Publications, 2005), *500 CC: Computer Citations* (London: King's College Publications, 2005).

studies or other walk of life, still you are going to need tools of mind. *Thought₂Talk* is a combination of a first aid kit with a manual to form a rudimentary toolbox for proper reflection and correct expression.

To benefit from *Thought₂Talk* over a few sessions you need to comply with what 'Norton the warden' says in the *The Shawshank Redemption*:

> I believe in two things—discipline and the bible. Here you will receive both: Put your trust in the Lord, your [...] belongs to me.

This also holds true here: For the next few hours, you need discipline, and furthermore, this is your bible and your [...] belongs to your instructor.

I would like to express my gratitude to John Symons and Klaus Frovin Jørgensen for many helpful suggestions and constructive comments and to Elizabeth Pando and Christopher M. Whalin for proof-reading the manuscript. Also I would like to thank my publisher **Automatic Press** ♦ $\frac{V}{I}$P, in particular senior publishing editor V.J. Menshy, for taking on this project.

Vincent F. Hendricks
Copenhagen
September 2006

Signs and Symbols

A few symbols are needed anyway, if not here, then anywhere while learning for life and not just studying for credits.

	Greek Alphabet		
1.	α	A	alpha
2.	β	B	beta
3.	γ	Γ	gamma
4.	δ	Δ	delta
5.	ε	E	epsilon
6.	ζ	Z	zeta
7.	η	H	eta
8.	θ	Θ	theta
9.	ι	I	iota
10.	κ	K	kappa
11.	λ	Λ	lambda
12.	μ	M	mu
13.	ν	N	nu
14.	ξ	Ξ	xi
15.	o	O	omicron
16.	π	Π	pi
17.	ρ	P	rho
18.	σ	Σ	sigma
19.	τ	T	tau
20.	υ	Y	upsilon
21.	ϕ	Φ	phi
22.	χ	X	chi
24.	ψ	Ψ	psi
25.	ω	Ω	omega

		Logic Symbols	
1.	$\neg$	not	negation
2.	$\wedge$	and	conjunction
3.	$\vee$	or	disjunction (inclusive)
4.	$\rightarrow$	if ... then	implication (material)
5.	$\leftrightarrow$	if and only if	biconditional implication
6.	$\underline{\vee}$	either or	disjunction (exclusive)
7.	$\Diamond$	possible	possibility operator
8.	$\Box$	necessary	necessity operator
9.	$\mapsto$	if it were ...then	counterfactual
10.	K_α	α knows that	epistemic operator
11.	B_α	α believes that	doxastic operator
12.	$\bot$	bottom	false
13.	$\top$	top	true
14.	$\therefore$	therefore	argument indicator
15.	$\models$	entails	semantic consequence

1

Statements

Eloquence is logic on fire.

—Lyman Beecher

The *declarative* statements of natural language of immediate interest for scrutinizing fundamental principles of thought fall crudely into three distinct categories.

In order to separate these categories a definition is required. A definition in general consists of what is to be defined, called the *definiendum*, and that which defines it, called the *definiens*, in such a way that definiendum and definiens provide *necessary* and *sufficient* conditions for each other.

The definition needed to separate the categories of interest may now be formulated accordingly:

Definition 1 The Principle of Bivalence: *Every statement of language is either true or false.*

The principle of bivalence entails that every statement of interest is either true or false, and if every statement of language is either true or false, then the principle of bivalence is satisfied. Thus definiendum and definiens provide necessary and sufficient conditions for each other. This is not to say that a natural language includes only declarative statements which are either true or false. Commands, aesthetic judgements and statements of moral viewpoints are not true or false in any obvious way but rather either speech acts or expressions of various sentiments. These meaningful but non-assortoric statements – non-assortoric in the sense that they are not assertions about a state of affairs – are excluded for now.[1]

According to the principle of bivalence, truth and falsity are properties of statements—and statements *only*. The principle suf-

---

[1] Instead of using the term 'statement', a better term to use would be 'proposition' which is a statement that is true or false. However, not to introduce too much terminology, statement is used with the above restriction.

fices for extracting the aforementioned categories of statements which in turn reflect certain characteristic patterns for thought to talk.

1.1 Contradictory Statements

In *Annie Hall*, Woody Allen says at some point in the movie:

$$\text{What if everything is an illusion?} \\ \text{Then I definitely overpaid for my carpet!} \tag{1.1}$$

If everything is an illusion as the first statement says, then there would be no such thing as purchasing a carpet, and thus he could not have overpaid for it. Something must go as the two statements are inconsistent with each other. In general, a set of statements is *inconsistent* if they cannot all be true at the same time. Conversely, a set of statements is *consistent* if they can all be true at the same time.

By claiming (1.1) Woody Allen is contradicting himself in an, admittedly, amusing way. As amusing as it may seem, contradictions are something the human mind does not handle too well. This has been well-known since at least Aristotle who gave the first explicit formulation of the principle of non-contradiction:

Definition 2 The Principle of Non-Contradiction: *'It is clear, then, that such a principle is the most certain of all and we can formulate it thus: It is impossible for the same thing at the same time to belong and not belong to the same thing at the same time and in the same respect.'*

Aristotle continues that violating the principle amounts to being 'nothing but a plant' unless one is willing to specify the way in which a thing is the same yet different.

Not too long ago, the following bumper-sticker was a very popular item to put on cars

$$\text{Honk, if your horn is broken} \tag{1.2}$$

which is as contradictory as

$$\text{Don't use contractions} \tag{1.3}$$

since it is going to be hard for you to honk if your horn is busted, as little as you can rule against using contractions when a contraction is used to formulate your rule. Although (1.2) and (1.3) may not be declarative statements in the strict sense (as they have a command component) they still have a contradictory ring to them.

Contradictions are statements for which there are no situations making true—they are notoriously false:

Definition 3 Contradiction: *A statement is a contradiction if it is false in all possible situations.*

The statement

$$\text{I'm going out and staying in} \tag{1.4}$$

is an immediate contradiction of the form 'A is the case and not-A is the case'. Which way is it going to be—you can't have it both ways unless you specify the way in which you are going out to a club and at the same time staying in to watch the latest episode of *Sex and the City*. Where (1.4) is a contradiction based on the *form* of the statement, the contradictory nature of (1.2) and (1.3) stems from the *meanings* of the words making up the sentences in question. Inconsistencies like (1.1) and contradictions like (1.2) and (1.3) may be amusing indeed but only because they are not to be taken seriously and convey no information.

US-Secretary of Defence, Donald Rumsfeld, is on the other hand to be taken seriously while conveying information. He is famous for being wordy—to the point of contradiction in fact like during the Department of Defence News Briefing on February 12, 2002:

> Reports that say that something hasn't happened are always interesting to me, because as we know, there are known knowns; there are things we know we know. We also know there are known unknowns; that is to say we know there are some things we do not know.

Everything is fine so far: Rumsfeld knows that he is standing on the press-podium of the White House, and by reflection he knows that he does; he also knows, say, that he does not know the train schedules for all the trains leaving Grand Central Station in New York City, so he knows that he does not know. Rumsfeld however continues

$$\text{But there are also unknown unknowns,} \atop \text{the ones we don't know we don't know.} \tag{1.5}$$

'Unknown unknowns' amounts to a contradiction by assertion—simply saying that there are things 'we don't know we don't know' is to have knowledge of unknowns which allegedly is unknowable. Thus, (1.5) reduces to the absurd. No wonder Rumsfeld goes on to 'cleverly' say:

> If I know the answer I'll tell you the answer, and if I don't, I'll just respond, cleverly.

Way before Rumsfeld, the American philosopher G.E. Moore (1873–1958) argued that there is something inadvertently contradictory about saying things like

$$\text{There are 9 planets in our solar system,} \atop \text{but it is not the case that I believe it.} \quad (1.6)$$

Even granted that (1.6) only involves an error or omission it all the same sounds self-contradictory given mere assertion. Any instance of (1.6) is nowadays referred to as a Moore-paradox—now, Rumsfeld should have known Moore.

An infamous example of a performative contradiction in American politics was provided by former Vice-President Dan Quayle in 1992 while he was visiting Trenton's Munoz Rivera School. A twelve year old school-boy, William Figueroa, had correctly spelled 'potato' on the black-board, but Quayle insisted on adding an 'e' to the end. Quayle ruefully reported on a Washington Post article that suggested the Trenton flub got such wide media coverage because 'it seemed like a perfect illustration of what people thought about me anyway.'

When under sufficient pressure in a debate, people tend to say: 'Well, yeah, you might be right, but then again ...'

$$\text{Everything is relative.} \quad (1.7)$$

If everything is relative then there must be something that everything is relative to. But this something cannot be relative, because otherwise relative would make no sense. Thus there must be something which is absolute, but then everything cannot be relative. Contradiction!

One should refrain from uttering contradictions—no information is conveyed, the human mind can't digest them at face value. Realize that in any dispute, one always attempts to catch the opponent in holding contradictory points of view. It is the ultimate knock-down argument because the opponent is in turn uttering something which is only and always false, and is hence back in the vegetative state.

1.2 Tautological Statements

Former US-Vice-President candidate Bob Dole once said:

> The Internet is a great way to get on the net. (1.8)

That is hard to disagree with especially if the Internet defines the net, then the Internet is *the* way to get on it. One might as well have said, '1 = 1,' or the 'Chrysler Building is the Chrysler Building.' As opposed to the contradictions above, (1.8) along with '1 = 1' and the 'Chrysler Building is the Chrysler Building' are all true in all possible situations. There are no situations which would make them false:

Definition 4 Tautology: *A statement is a tautology if it is true in all possible situations.*

Always true, tautologies are *not* very informative because they are impossible to falsify. They are somewhat like uttering 'uh-hu'—that is always appropriate in any exchange independently of whether you agree or disagree with whatever is being said. The possible uninformative plain noise nature, adding no information, of tautologies is quintessentially exemplified by the statement prefices

> It goes without saying that ... (1.9)

and

> Needless to say ... . (1.10)

Where (1.8) is a tautology based on the meaning of the words, some statements are tautologies given their form. The statement

> Either it rains or it doesn't (1.11)

is true when it rains, but it is also true when it doesn't, and in the movie *Deer Hunter* Robert De Niro replies to his co-star John Cazale

> This is this, this ain't something else, this is this. (1.12)

Later in *Heat* – during their only face-to-face meeting at the highway coffee-shop – De Niro replies similarly to Al Pacino on Pacino's question of whether De Niro's way of life in the movie is 'pretty vague':

$$\text{It is what it is.} \quad (1.13)$$

Both (1.8) and (1.13) are tautologies of the form '$A = A$'; (1.11) is of the form 'A is the case or not-A is the case', while (1.12) is subsumed under 'If A is the case, then A is the case' given that the statement is interpreted as 'If it is this, then it is this'.

Tautological statements which are true simply by virtue of the meanings of the words involved are called *analytic a priori* statements. Woody Allen has one:

> I don't want to achieve immortality through my work—
> I want to achieve it through not dying.

$$(1.14)$$

By scrutiny of the meaning of the words in which immortality defines not dying the statement is analytic and it is *a priori* since it is not required to consult experience to settle the truth-value. Similarly, the British pop-band Human League has a song with the lyrics

> I believe in truth, so I lie a lot

which may likewise be interpreted as an *analytic a priori* statement since lying is impossible to define without a concept of truth, as little as truth makes any sense sense without a notion of not truth-telling, i.e. lying.

It is generally considered a virtue to say something true, but tautologies are not quite it. To say something true and informative is really virtuous. It allows for action, deliberation and decision rather than leaving interlocutors and their thoughts with the apathy of contradictions and tautologies given their lack of information either by being always false, or by being always true.

1.3 Contingent Statements

The statement

$$\text{It rained in New York City on October 24, 2005} \quad (1.15)$$

is either true or false—true if it did rain in the city on that date and false if it did not. Contingent statement may be either true or false. First Lady of the Philippines, Imelda Marcos, married to president Ferdinand Marcos and his regime which was overthrown in 1986, Minister of Human Settlements and Governor of Metro Manila and affectionately called 'Mother of the Nation,' had over 3,000 pairs of shoes (size 8 1/2) – and her collection additionally included a pair of plastic disco sandals with three-inch-high, flashing, battery-operated heels; 500 (size 38) brassieres; 200 (size 42) girdles and a bulletproof bra – in her closet once proclaimed:

$$I \text{ am beyond logic and rationality.} \quad (1.16)$$

The statement has the virtue of being possibly true and possibly false, or true in certain situations and false in others. Either way, given the circumstances, (1.16) is a bold statement which takes the chance of being proved correct as well as incorrect:

Definition 5 Contingent statement: *A statement is contingent if it is true in some situations and false in other situations.*

Contingent statements are interesting as they carry information about the world and its state of affairs. They leave room for genuine disagreement, rather than the trivial disagreement given contradictions or the trivial agreement in light of tautologies. On February 5, 2003 Former US Secretary of State,Colin Powell, addressed the UN Security Council with the following contingent set of statements about Iraq:

$$\begin{array}{l}\text{With this track record, Iraqi denials}\\ \text{of supporting terrorism take the place}\\ \text{alongside the other Iraqi denials} \quad (1.17)\\ \text{of weapons of mass destruction.}\\ \text{It is all a web of lies.}\end{array}$$

This turned out to be false—at least the part about hiding weapons of mass destruction. But it could have been true—which seems at least pretty close to the subsequent line of thought exercised by the US Administration after the statement above, and more like them, were refuted. All the same (1.17) was bold, to the extent that Powell soon enough was expedited out of office.

The word Iraq is not in and by itself synonymous with weapons of mass destruction and terrorism as little as the meaning of the words Imelda Marcos transcends logic and rationality *per se*. Both (1.16) and (1.17) are *synthetic a posteriori* statements as analyses of meaning do not suffice for settling their truth-values and consultations with experience, i.e. observations, are required.

Contingent statements are important building blocks in constructing pertinent real-life arguments. Either they may serve as premises for conclusions or are conclusions in their own right derived from other statements of mostly a contingent nature.

In the next chapter it will become apparent that the key property of arguments is their *validity*. Besides validity they may also be sound, i.e. their premises are factually true. Powell and the US Administration may have constructed shelves and shelves worth of valid arguments in favor of their stance, but their premises were not factually true, thus the arguments may have all been valid but not sound. That's what evidence – or lack of evidence – showed. Providing true premises for arguments is where disagreement typically arises as Isaac Asimov describes:

> ... My answer to him was, '... when people thought the Earth was flat, they were wrong. When people thought the Earth was spherical they were wrong. But if you think that thinking the Earth is spherical is just as wrong as thinking the Earth is flat, then your view is wronger than both of them put together.'

A note of caution. Asimov uses 'right' and 'wrong' as roughly equivalent to 'true' and 'false'. This is fine as long as it is clear from the context what they are taken to mean, but in general these two distinctions should not be equivocated among. 'I'm digesting yesterday's meal' is true or false; asking whether it is right or wrong in any other sense than true or false, say in a moral sense, seems off the mark.

To recap, statements are true or false, not right or wrong, of the world. By way of example, it is true that the rain forest is being cut down, but this is normally not considered to be right as it may have dire consequences for the ecosystem. Some might at the same time find it acceptable, otherwise the peasants in the Amazons have to go back to growing coca leaves for narcotics production and civilized consumption. It is false that abortion is legal worldwide, and that may meet with some's religious convictions. Others might find it wrong that it is not legalized since world legalization of abortion may save the world from being over-populated. It is also a fact that not all Chinese have cars; right to some because a car for every Chinese would be a severe health-hazard for the planet and its inhabitants because of the extra pollution. Then again, wrong to others because the Chinese should enjoy the fruit of civilization as much as the Western world.

The world may tell us whether statements are true or false, depending on whether the statements describe a state of affairs or not—that may from time to time be hard enough to determine. The world is secretive or underdetermined that way ever so often. All the same, truth and falsity are descriptive notions, whereas right and wrong are normative or evaluative notions which the world does not settle in any immediate way.

1.4 Nasty Statements

The expressability of natural language is impressive. With it one may formulate declaratives ('The NYSE index for frozen concentrated orange juice is rising'), presumptives ('I think or believe the NYSE index for frozen concentrated orange juice is rising'), interrogatives ('Is the NYSE index for frozen concentrated orange juice rising?'), counterfactuals ('If it were the case that the NYSE index for frozen concentrated orange juice is rising, I would buy myself an Aston Martin Volante'), deontics ('The NYSE index for frozen concentrated orange juice is obligated to rise'), express emotion, distress, happiness, opinions etc. The expressability of natural language is a virtue as well as a vice.

Language exhibits malignant features that may confuse thought, action, deliberation. Consider the statement

$$\text{This sentence is false.} \qquad (1.18)$$

If the principle of bivalence holds, then (1.18) should be true or false. If (1.18) is true, then (1.18) is false. Suppose now that it is false. Then that is exactly what (1.18) says, so it is true. It has accordingly been demonstrated that (1.18) is true if and only if it is false. Since (1.18) is one or the other, it is both. Contradiction! This is known as the Liar Paradox—try going through the steps with 'I'm lying' and in the end you will find the same paradox. It has been the center of attention of philosophers, logicians, mathematicians and linguistics for nearly 2500 years.

There are many variations over this paradoxical theme and they all in one way or the other involve self-reference like

$$\text{If I were you, who would be reading this sentence?}$$

or

$$\text{Do you read me?}$$

or

> Only one thing is certain—that is, nothing is certain.

If this statement is true, it is also false. Or how about Raymond Smullyan's potentially insulting version

> Only an idiot would believe this sentence.

It is not the time nor the place to pursue the discussion of self-reference which is vast, complicated and interesting—there are drugs for self-reference and some of the paradoxes it generates. Here it suffices to say that due to the problematic nature of such statements some have thought that natural language is too rich – and too inconsistent – to be the proper medium for thought and that only restricted parts of language are suitable vehicles for proper reasoning.

2
Arguments

> I'm sorry to say that the subject I most disliked was mathematics. I have thought about it. I think the reason was that mathematics leaves no room for argument. If you made a mistake, that was all there was to it.
>
> —Malcolm X

A simple yet crisp and concise explanation of what an argument is stems from Monty Python's *Argument Clinic* sketch:

Definition 6 Argument: *'An argument is a connected series of statements intended to establish a definite proposition.'*

True or false statements in themselves are not arguments, they are just claims. Claims may however be justified and offering an argument is to offer a series of related statements which represent an attempt to justify the claim in question. The central question is what it would take for the opponent to buy the claim set forth—or what justificational force is required for the opponent to believe that what is being claimed is true rather than false.

The most compelling justification would be to show that the opponent is obligated to accept the claim on pain of otherwise being a plant. That is, to demonstrate that the claim follows from a set of premises in such that a way, that if the premises are true, then the conclusion must be true and the opponent's failure to acknowledge this involves a contradiction. That is the essence of *valid* arguments and the objects of this chapter and the next.

Other justifications for believing a claim would be brute force, fear, compassion, popular opinion, ... Brute force and bulldozing can be very effective vehicles for getting people to believe but has very little to do with truth and validity. Being convinced because of truth is *logical*, being convinced because of something else, is something else (see chapter 4).

2. Arguments

2.1 Argument Schemata

As users (and abusers) of thought and talk, humans are capable of logical inferences and identification of such inferences. Here is one:

1. <u>If</u> the Americans are invading China, <u>then</u> the world is at war.

2. The world is <u>not</u> at war.

3. Therefore: The Americans are <u>not</u> invading China.

Statements (1) and (2) are called the *premises* whereas statement (3) is referred to as the *conclusion* of the argument. The expression 'therefore', which from now on will be written as '∴' indicates that a certain relation obtains between premises and conclusion in such a way that if the premises are accepted, then one is forced to accept the conclusion. Other terms than 'therefore' are used to indicate this relationship like 'hence', 'thus', 'consequently' and so forth.

The argument above is valid since without contradiction one cannot accept the premises and yet refrain from accepting the conclusion. Additionally, the validity is dependent on the connector words underlined. If the statements about an American invasion, China and the war of the world are substituted for other statements, but the connector words are kept intact and in place, the result is a new valid inference or deduction of the same *form* but with a different content:

1. <u>If</u> Sting loves somebody, <u>then</u> they are to be set free.

2. They are <u>not</u> to be set free.

3. ∴ It is <u>not</u> the case that Sting loves somebody.

The logical validity of the inferences depends entirely on the logical form of the arguments and not their content. The logical form is determined by the connectors 'if ..., then ...' and 'not ...'. This gives the following *argument schema*:

1. <u>If</u> A, <u>then</u> B.

2. <u>Not</u> B.

3. ∴ <u>Not</u> A.

2. Arguments   13

For the proper choice of A and B the two arguments above reappear. An arbitrary valid argument may thus be defined as being an *instance of a logically valid argument schema*.

Here is another argument which immediately is recognized as valid:

1. If you are drawing a caricature of somone, then you insult them.

2. You are drawing a caricature of somone.

3. ∴ You insult them.

The argument is an instance of another schema:

1. If A, then B.

2. A.

3. ∴ B.

Now the connectors 'not' and 'if ..., then ...' play a decisive role for logical form but so do words like 'and' and 'or':

1. Either the Muhammad-drawings are bad taste, or the Muhammad-drawings are expressions of the freedom of speech.

2. The Muhammad-drawings are not expressions of the freedom of speech.

3. ∴ The Muhammad-drawings are bad taste.

This argument is an instance of the argument schema:

1. Either A or B.

2. Not B.

3. ∴ A.

Now one is free to disagree with the argument about the drawings of the prophet, but one cannot disagree with the conclusion if one accepts the premises. Well one can of course, but the price paid is high—reduction to a plant. In order to disagree one has to show that one or more of the premises are false. That will get somewhere, and when people disagree but acknowledge the strength of valid arguments it is usually about whether the premises (contingent statements) are in fact true. An argument may be valid but not *sound* in the sense of the premises being actually true. A good argument is one which enjoys both qualities—validity and soundness.

The following argument:

1. It is not the case, that the Muhammad-drawings are bad taste and that the Muhammad-drawings are expressions of the freedom of speech.

2. The Muhammad-drawings are bad taste.

3. ∴ The Muhammad-drawings are not expressions of the freedom of speech.

This argument can be recast as the schema:

1. Not (A and B).

2. A.

3. ∴ Not B.

Statements constructed from 'if ..., then ...' are called *material* implications, as there are other forms of implication than the material one in natural language. Another connector is obtained by letting the material implication go both ways, $A \to B$ and $B \to A$, which is also written as $A \leftrightarrow B$ and read 'A, if, and only if, B.' Statements constructed from '..., if, and only if,, ...' are called *bi-implications*. If the statements are constructed from 'not', 'and' and 'or', they are called *negations, conjunctions* and *disjunctions* respectively. The underlined connector words are called *logical connectives*, and the following standard short-hands are introduced for them:

$\to$ for 'if ..., then ...'   (implication)

$\leftrightarrow$ for '..., if and only if, ...'   (bi-implication)

$\neg$ for 'not'   (negation)

$\wedge$ for 'and'   (conjunction)

$\vee$ for 'or'   (disjunction)

The system of statements introduced is called the *propositional language* as what is formalized are entire propositions (or statements that are true for false) rather than the words that make them up.

2. Arguments

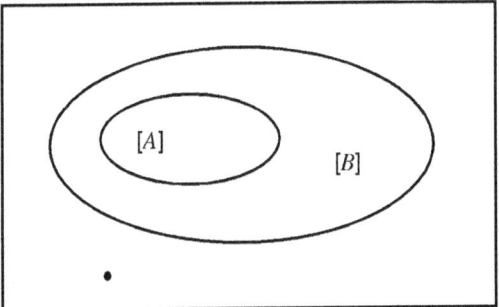

FIGURE 2.1. Modus (Tollendo) Tollens.

With the new set of symbols, the argument schemata may be represented in a compact fashion. The first schema:

1. If A, then B.
2. Not B.
3. ∴ Not A.

looks like this:

1. $A \to B$
2. $\neg B$ (Modus Tollens)
3. ∴ $\neg A$

The schema is called *Modus (Tollendo) Tollens*, and is always a logically valid inference no matter what A and B refers to.

To say that Modus Tollens is always a logically valid inference is a bold statement. That needs to be *proved*: So let $[A]$ denote all the situations making A true, and let $[B]$ denote all the situations making B true. A implies B means, that if A is true, then B is true. In this case, all the situations making A true, will also make B true, so the set $[A]$ will be contained in the set $[B]$. Given the first premise, the following holds

$$[A] \subseteq [B],$$

which means that $[A]$ is a *subset* of $[B]$. Premise 2 says that $\neg B$ is the case, but if $[A]$ is contained in $[B]$, as premise 1 prescribes, then the actual situation (marked '•' in figure 2.1) described in premise 2 cannot be an element of $[B]$. Then the actual situation cannot be in $[A]$ as $[A]$ is a subset of $[B]$ which exactly is the message of the conclusion and figure 2.1.

Similarly

16   2. Arguments

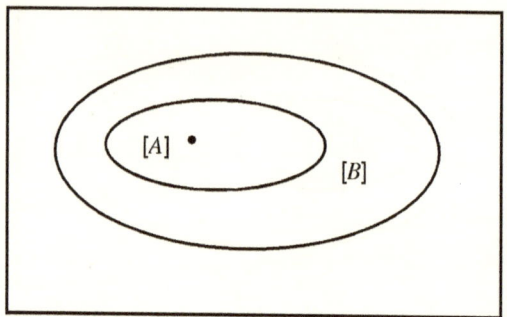

FIGURE 2.2. Modus (Ponendo) Ponens.

1. If A, then B.
2. A.
3. ∴ B.

may be written as:

    1. $A \rightarrow B$
    2. A (Modus Ponens)
    3. ∴ B

This argument schema is called *Modus (Ponendo) Ponens*. Again, let [A] denote all the situations in which A is true, and let [B] refer to all the situations in which B is true. In the first premise $A \rightarrow B$ means that if A is true, so is B, or $[A] \subseteq [B]$. Since the second premise says that A is the case, i.e. that the actual situation '•' is an element of [A], which is written $• \in [A]$, then the actual situation must also be in [B], as the conclusion claims and is revealed in figure 2.2.

What has just been proved again is that no matter A and B denote, Modus Ponens will remain a logically valid argument schema

The third argument schema

1. Either A or B.
2. Not B.
3. ∴ A.

may be written as

    1. $A \lor B$
    2. $\neg B$ (Modus Tollendo Ponens)
    3. ∴ A

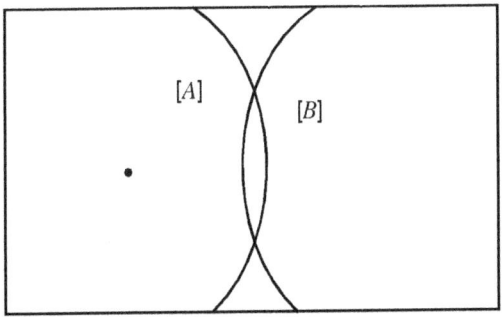

FIGURE 2.3. Modus Tollendo Ponens.

and is called *Modus Tollendo Ponens*. The first premise says that $A \vee B$ holds, which is the same as saying that every situation either is a member of $[A]$ or $[B]$. There are no situations outside $[A]$ or $[B]$. Hence the *union*, $[A] \cup [B]$, contains the actual situation. The second premise says that $\neg B$ is the case, and so the actual situation cannot be in $[B]$, i.e. • $\notin [B]$, which in turns means that the actual situation is a member of $[A]$, or • $\in [A]$. This is precisely what both the conclusion and figure 2.3 convey.

The final argument schema

1. Not (A and B).

2. A.

3. ∴ Not B.

may be formalized as

1. $\neg(A \wedge B)$
2. A (Modus Ponendo Tollens)
3. ∴ $\neg B$

The schema is called *Modus Ponendo Tollens*. The first premise carries the message that there are no situations making both A and B true, so the *intersection*, $[A] \cap [B]$, of all the situations making both A and B true is empty. The sets $[A]$ and $[B]$ are disjoint and share no situations. This entails that when premise 2 says that the actual situation is in $[A]$, then it is not in $[B]$, which the conclusion says and figure 2.4 shows.

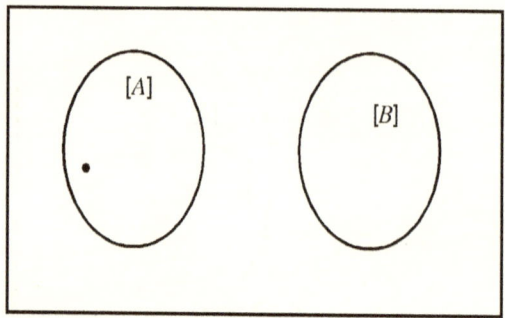

FIGURE 2.4. Modus Ponendo Tollens.

2.2 Syntax and Semantics

Statements which do not contain logical connectives are called *atomic statements*. Statements A and B in the argument schemata are examples of atomics. Complex statements are constructed by starting out with the atomic statements and then conjoining them using the logical connectives in accordance with certain syntactic conditions. The *syntax* initially specifies what the alphabet of the language consists of:

1. *A collection of propositional symbols* $\mathbf{p}_1, \mathbf{p}_2, \mathbf{p}_3, \ldots$ *(standing for atomic statements)*
2. *Parentheses '(', ')'.*
3. *The logical connectives* $\neg, \wedge, \vee, \rightarrow, \leftrightarrow$.

Just like a grammar for any language, syntactic rules are required in order to specify what *well-formed* (and meaningful) statements of the propositional language are:

1. *If A is a propositional symbol, then A is a well-formed statement.*
2. *If A is a well-formed statement, then $\neg A$ is a well-formed statement.*
3. *If A and B are well-formed statements, then $(A \wedge B), (A \vee B), (A \rightarrow B)$ and $(A \leftrightarrow B)$ are well-formed statements.*

Thus, a statement like

$$((A \wedge B) \rightarrow A) \leftrightarrow B \qquad (2.1)$$

is well-formed while $(\wedge AB \rightarrow \leftrightarrow B)$ is not. Note that the parentheses are used to specify what *scopes* the logical connectives of (2.1) have. The conjunction has the smallest scope in (2.1) as it only ranges over $(A \wedge B)$, the implication has a larger scope as it ranges over $(A \wedge B) \rightarrow A$, while the bi-implication is the main connective as it has range over the entire statement (2.1). The scope of logical connectives is an integral part of determining the logical form of statements in which the connectives occur.

Every logically correct inference or valid argument is dependent on a set of situations under which the statements making up the inference or argument are true or false. To specify these situations in which the given statements are true or false, and thus give a *model* for the assignment of truth-values is to provide a *semantics*. The validity of the argument schemata were found to be intimately connected to the way in which the statements comprising the arguments were constructed out of the atomic statements and the logical connectives and consequently the logical form of the statements involved. Uncovering logical form is tantamount to specifying the truth-conditions for the statements in question.

In logic one is generally interested in uncovering whether it is logically correct to infer from a number of premises $A_1, \ldots, A_n$ to a conclusion K, where the A's and the K are statements formulated in the propositional language (or extended versions hereof of which there are many). Logical consequence or valid inference is the cornerstone of logic. The following definition of validity is the single most important definition in understanding thought as well as talk:

Definition 7 Validity: *K follows from premises $A_1, \ldots, A_n$ means that K's truth is a consequence of the premises' truth. Put differently, it is impossible to have a situation in which all the premises are true but the conclusion yet false.*

When the conclusion K follows logically from the premises listed $A_1, \ldots, A_n$ in accordance with definition (7) write

$$A_1, \ldots, A_n \models K. \qquad (2.2)$$

The symbol '$\models$' is called the *semantical turnstile* and (2.2) is referred to as a *semantic consequence*. If K does not follow from $A_1, \ldots, A_n$ write '$\not\models$'.

If one has to show that K follows from the premises one has to demonstrate that no matter how the truth of the involved statements varies the conclusion will always be true when the premises

2. Arguments

are true. Similarly one may also show that an argument is invalid by finding *a situation in which all the premises are true yet the conclusion false*.

According to the principle of bivalence from chapter 1 it is assumed that every statement of interest is either true, denoted by the symbol '$\top$' and called 'top', or false denoted by the symbol '$\bot$' called 'bottom'. Another principle – one of compositionality – also holds:

Definition 8 Principle of Compositionality: *The truth-value of a complex statement A in a situation is uniquely determined by the truth-values of the statements making up A using the logical connectives.*

Thus an arbitrary statement A is either $\top$ or $\bot$ and if A is a complex statement, its truth-value is fixed by its parts and the truth-functional behavior of the logical connectives.

The truth-functional behavior given by the truth-conditions for the negation $\neg A$ may be listed in the following *truth-table*:

Negation

A	$\neg A$
$\top$	$\bot$
$\bot$	$\top$

The negation, $\neg A$, of an arbitrary statement A is true when A is false, and false whenever A is true.

Conjunction and disjunction have the truth-tables:

Conjunction

A	B	$A \wedge B$
$\top$	$\top$	$\top$
$\top$	$\bot$	$\bot$
$\bot$	$\top$	$\bot$
$\bot$	$\bot$	$\bot$

Disjunction

A	B	$A \vee B$
$\top$	$\top$	$\top$
$\top$	$\bot$	$\top$
$\bot$	$\top$	$\top$
$\bot$	$\bot$	$\bot$

A conjunction is only true in the case in which both conjuncts A and B are true and false otherwise.

The disjunction described is *inclusive*. It is true in all situations save the situation in which both disjuncts A and B are false. The natural usage of 'or' is quite often understood this way. When asking Milton who is 6 years old whether he wants ice cream or a Hershey's candy bar for desert chances are that he will answer with a simple 'yes'. His strategy is to interpret the 'or' as inclusive which leaves open the possibility of getting both ice cream and the candy bar for desert. The intention of the question is of course that you can't eat the cake and have it too, so Milton may either have ice cream or the candy bar but not both. If the disjunction is viewed in this light it is called *exclusive* since it slams the door shut on the situation in which the disjunction is true when both disjuncts are true. The exclusive 'or', sometimes written '$\underline{\vee}$' has different truth-functional properties and hence a truth-table different from the inclusive 'or'. All the same it is possible to define the exclusive disjunction in terms of the logical connectives already present so there is no need to introduce it explicitly.

The material implication has the following truth-conditions:

Material implication

A	B	$A \to B$
$\top$	$\top$	$\top$
$\top$	$\bot$	$\bot$
$\bot$	$\top$	$\top$
$\bot$	$\bot$	$\top$

The only case in which the material implication is false is the one where the *antecedent* A is true, but the *consequent* B false. That makes good sense because

If Dickie C eats arsenic, then he dies

is clearly false if Dickie C actually consumes arsenic, but does not die from the intake. Eating arsenic is a *sufficient condition* for dying. It is conversely not immediately clear that

If Dickie C is an amoeba, then he has an IQ of 250

is true, since it is false that Dickie C is an amoeba, and he for sure does not have an IQ of 250 and so the consequent is false too, and even had he had an IQ of 250, but still not being an amoeba, the material implication is true all the same.

It is contestable whether the last two rows of the truth-table are faithful representations of the natural language implication. First of all, natural language has more than one form of implication— that is the reason why the one above is called the *material* implication. Second, for a great many purposes the material implication turns out to be an adequate formal translation for a variety of natural language implications. There are also a set of formal logical reasons why the material implication looks the way it does but that will be kept secret for a rainy day.

The bi-implication is true in those cases where A and B are true, and where A and B are false—A and B are necessary and sufficient conditions for each other.

Bi-implication

A	B	$A \leftrightarrow B$
$\top$	$\top$	$\top$
$\top$	$\bot$	$\bot$
$\bot$	$\top$	$\bot$
$\bot$	$\bot$	$\top$

It was mentioned that one may define the exclusive disjunction '$\underline{\vee}$' using the connectives already introduced. This is quite so because $A \underline{\vee} B$ and $\neg(A \leftrightarrow B)$ have the same truth-table:

A	B	$A \leftrightarrow B$	$\neg(A \leftrightarrow B)$	$A \underline{\vee} B$
$\top$	$\top$	$\top$	$\bot$	$\bot$
$\top$	$\bot$	$\bot$	$\top$	$\top$
$\bot$	$\top$	$\bot$	$\top$	$\top$
$\bot$	$\bot$	$\top$	$\bot$	$\bot$

The negation of the bi-implication precisely describes the truth-functional behavior for the exclusive disjunction. Two statements A and B are called *logically equivalent*, when they have the same truth-table and thus exhibit the same truth-functional behavior. Logically equivalent statements A, B are written

$$A \equiv B. \tag{2.3}$$

Another couple of logically equivalent statements is the material implication $A \to B$ and its *contraposition*

$$\neg B \to \neg A$$

which again is revealed in the truth-table:

A	B	$\neg A$	$\neg B$	$\neg B \to \neg A$
$\top$	$\top$	$\bot$	$\bot$	$\top$
$\top$	$\bot$	$\bot$	$\top$	$\bot$
$\bot$	$\top$	$\top$	$\bot$	$\top$
$\bot$	$\bot$	$\top$	$\top$	$\top$

2. Arguments   23

Natural language is rich in connectives, besides the ones already looked at, consider:

- '_ unless _'

- '_ but _'

- '_ given _'

- '_ insofar _'

- '_ on condition of _'

- '_ whenever _'

- ...

A bunch of these connectives can be formalized using the logical connectives as their natural semantics are close enough to the formal semantics to warrant formalization.

A but B	$A \wedge B$
A however B	$A \wedge B$
A unless B	$\neg B \to A$
B only if A	$B \to A$
given B then A	$B \to A$
A in case B	$B \to A$
A depending on B	$B \to A$
A is necessary for B	$B \to A$
A is sufficient for B	$A \to B$
A whenever B	$A \leftrightarrow B$

2.3 Back to Statements

Revisit the three statement types of chapter 1 and consider the following statements and their truth-value assignments given the truth-tables for the logical connectives $\neg, \wedge, \vee \rightarrow$:

$$A \wedge \neg A$$

A	$\neg A$	$A \wedge \neg A$
$\top$	$\bot$	$\bot$
$\bot$	$\top$	$\bot$

1.

$$A \vee \neg A$$

A	$\neg A$	$A \vee \neg A$
$\top$	$\bot$	$\top$
$\bot$	$\top$	$\top$

2.

$$A \rightarrow \neg A$$

A	$\neg A$	$A \rightarrow \neg A$
$\top$	$\bot$	$\bot$
$\bot$	$\top$	$\top$

3.

The statement of the *form*

1. $A \wedge \neg A$ is *always false* (and of the same form as 1.2, 1.3, 1.4)

2. $A \vee \neg A$ is *always true* (and of the same form as 1.11), while

3. $A \rightarrow \neg A$ is *sometimes true and sometimes false.*

The truth-tables is accordingly a procedure for testing whether something is a contradiction, tautology or contingent statement as:

1. *A statement is a* contradiction *if the last column of the truth-table only includes* $\bot$.

2. *A statement is a* tautology *if the last column of the truth-table only includes* $\top$.

3. *A statement is* contingent *if the last column of the truth-table includes both* $\top$ *and* $\bot$.

It gets better than that. Truth-tables may be used as a procedure for checking whether an argument is valid in accordance with definition (7). Go to the next chapter to see how that plays out.

3

Validities

If you go in for an argument, take care of your temper. Your logic, if you have any, will take care of itself. —Anonymous

---

Checking an argument for validity is dependent upon uncovering the logical form of the statements making up the argument's premises and conclusion. Once the form has been uncovered, one has to check whether definition (7) holds for the argument presented. It is easy to loose sight of what is what, so a procedure is needed to discover logical form and a procedure is needed to check for validity.

3.1 Strip to Discover

In daily debates and exchanges of opinion arguments are usually not presented in nice and easily accessible schemata formalized by letters and connectives. They are dressed up in fancy garments with complicated sentence structures, sexy expressions, cool stuff, sometimes involving tacit premises, noise in the background, booze, ladies and studs, the desire to impress and so forth making it less transparent whether there is an argument around at all, and if so, whether it is valid:

> Man, listen to me now will ya? Damn it! Where is my woman?—and give me a beer – Bud Light preferably – and I'll tell you who's what! History has shown that either economic inequality or religious differences are the reasons for people beating each other to a pulp. If a difference in religious convictions is the reason, then the commandment of loving your neighbor has failed. But then again, if humanity is not hateful by nature, then the commandment of loving your fellow man is not down the tubes. So dig this buddy! Either humanity is hateful or history has shown that economic

inequality is the reason for people beating each other to a pulp. How do ya' feel about that—ya' dig?

To investigate whether an argument is valid or not, strip it ... and discover logical form if there is any to be found. Discovering logical form is called *formalization*. Here is the manual to undress any argument:

1. *Identify the premises and the conclusion*: The conclusion is often marked by 'therefore', 'thus', 'hence' or some other word which indicates that something follows from something else.

    (a) In this case, the conclusion is what comes after 'So dig this buddy!'

2. *Identify the atomic statements in the argument and establish a 'key of translation'*, where the atomic statements are assigned propositional variables. Lower case letters are used to indicate that specific statements are being formalized.

    (a) p: History has shown that economic inequality is the reason for people beating each other to a pulp.
    (b) q: History has shown that religious differences is the reason for people beating each other to a pulp.
    (c) s: The commandment of loving your neighbor is intact.
    (d) t: Humanity is hateful.

3. *Identify the* main *logical connectives featuring in the premises and conclusion and uncover the logical form of the statements. In this particular case it seems to come down to the following dropping the 'Yo man, ya' dig bro'-noise.*

    (a) History has shown that economic inequality is the reason for people beating each other to a pulp $\vee$ History has shown that religious differences is the reason for people beating each other to a pulp.
    (b) History has shown that religious differences is the reason for people beating each other to a pulp $\rightarrow \neg$The commandment of loving your neighbor is intact.
    (c) $\neg$ Humanity is hateful $\rightarrow$ The commandment of loving your neighbor is intact.

(d) Therefore: Humanity is hateful ∨ History has shown that economic inequality is the reason for people beating each other to a pulp.

4. *Formalize*:

   (a) $p \vee q$
   (b) $q \to \neg s$
   (c) $\neg t \to s$
   (d) $\therefore t \vee p$

5. *Write up the semantical consequence*:

$$p \vee q, q \to \neg s, \neg t \to s \models t \vee p. \qquad (3.1)$$

It should be noted that there is no unequivocal answer as to how one should formalize everyday arguments. They are open to interpretation because the statements involved in them are open to interpretation. Sometimes the logical connectives only scratch the surface of what is really being said partly because expressions of natural language may also be context-sensitive. The rule of thumb is to study any argument with a principle of rational charity in hand, making as much logical sense of it as one can. Admittedly this may seem too friendly a favor from time to time as the Canadian educator and writer Laurence J. Peter once said:

Against logic there is no armor like ignorance.

3.2 Truth-Tables to Check

A tautology is a statement which is true no matter what. True no matter what is equivalent to saying that a tautology is an argument which is valid on empty premises. This is the reason why a tautology in general is written $\models A$ for an arbitrary statement A. The truth-table from the previous chapter

$$A \vee \neg A$$

A	$\neg A$	$A \vee \neg A$
⊤	⊥	⊤
⊥	⊤	⊤

2.

is actually a semantical demonstration of the fact that

$$\models A \vee \neg A. \tag{3.2}$$

Truth-tables furnish a procedure to check arguments for their validity. The number of rows in the truth-table is dependent on the number of atomic statements involved in the argument. In general, the length of a truth-table will be 2^n where n is the number of atomic statements in the argument and 2 is explained by the fact every statement is either true or false. Since there is only one atomic statement in (3.2), the number of rows is $2^1 = 2$.

Reconsider the semantical consequence resulting from formalization of the argument above:

$$p \vee q, q \to \neg s, \neg t \to s \models t \vee p.$$

The number of atomic statements in (3.1) is 4—in turn the number of rows is $2^4 = 16$. In order to exhaust all possible combinations of truth-value assignments to the atomic statements, the truth-value assignments in the columns alternate by division of 2 towards the right.

p	q	s	t	$p \vee q$	$q \to \neg s$	$\neg t \to s$	$t \vee p$
T	T	T	T	T	⊥	T	T
T	T	T	⊥	T	⊥	T	T
T	T	⊥	T	T	T	T	T
T	T	⊥	⊥	T	T	⊥	T
T	⊥	T	T	T	T	T	T
T	⊥	T	⊥	T	T	T	T
T	⊥	⊥	T	T	T	T	T
T	⊥	⊥	⊥	T	T	⊥	T
⊥	T	T	T	T	⊥	T	T
⊥	T	T	⊥	T	⊥	T	⊥
⊥	T	⊥	T	T	T	T	T
⊥	T	⊥	⊥	T	T	⊥	⊥
⊥	⊥	T	T	⊥	T	T	T
⊥	⊥	T	⊥	⊥	T	T	⊥
⊥	⊥	⊥	T	⊥	T	T	T
⊥	⊥	⊥	⊥	⊥	T	⊥	⊥

— In accordance with definition (7) of validity it be must checked whether there are any situations in which all the premises are true but the conclusion false.

3. Validities   29

— There are no such situations since in those situations in which the conclusion is false at least one of the premises is false as well.

— The semantical consequence is thus valid.

A conclusion K is a semantical consequence of the premises $A_1, ..., A_n$, if and only if, $A_1 \wedge ... \wedge A_n \to K$ is a tautology. In other words

$$A_1, ..., A_n \models K, \text{ if and only if, } \models A_1 \wedge ... \wedge A_n \to K.$$

On this basis it is possible to check whether (3.1) is a tautology by constructing a truth-table for

$$\models (((p \vee q) \wedge (q \to \neg s)) \wedge (\neg t \to s)) \to t \vee p \qquad (3.3)$$

Before moving on, note the use of parentheses – without them it is not possible to tell what the main connective and its scope is – as opposed to the sub-connectives and their scopes. In

$$\models p \vee q \wedge q \to \neg s \wedge \neg t \to s \to t \vee p$$

it is not clear whether the statement should be read as, say,

$$\models (p \vee (((q \wedge q) \to (\neg s \wedge \neg t))) \to (s \to t)) \vee p$$

or for instance

$$\models (p \vee q) \wedge (((q \to \neg s) \wedge \neg t) \to (s \to (t \vee p)))$$

and so on, none of which have the same meaning, nor the same truth-conditions as (3.3). The use of parentheses makes the statements unequivocal and prevents them for being open to interpretation.

It is now time to check (3.3) for validity.

3. Validities

p	q	s	t	$p \vee q$	$\wedge$	$q \rightarrow \neg s$	$\wedge$	$\neg t \rightarrow s$	$\rightarrow$	$t \vee p$
T	T	T	T	T	⊥	⊥				T
T	T	T	⊥	T	⊥	⊥				T
T	T	⊥	T	T	T	T				T
T	T	⊥	⊥	T	T	⊥				T
T	⊥	T	T	T	T	T				T
T	⊥	T	⊥	T	T	T				T
T	⊥	⊥	T	T	T	T				T
T	⊥	⊥	⊥	T	T	⊥				T
⊥	T	T	T	T	⊥	⊥				T
⊥	T	T	⊥	T	⊥	⊥				T
⊥	T	⊥	T	T	T	T				T
⊥	T	⊥	⊥	T	T	⊥				T
⊥	⊥	T	T	⊥	⊥	⊥				T
⊥	⊥	T	⊥	⊥	⊥	⊥				T
⊥	⊥	⊥	T	⊥	⊥	⊥				T
⊥	⊥	⊥	⊥	⊥	⊥	⊥				T

There exists no situation in which (3.3) is false and hence

$$\models (((p \vee q) \wedge (q \rightarrow \neg s)) \wedge (\neg t \rightarrow s)) \rightarrow t \vee p.$$

is a tautology. It is illuminating that behind all the gung-ho 'Yo-cuz-I-got-a-message-for-you-which-is-important' lies a tautology with a message as informative as '1 = 1'! That would have been hard to see without the formalization and the truth-tables to check.

Return to the original semantical consequence (3.1). There is only one way in which the conclusion of

$$p \vee q, q \rightarrow \neg s, \neg t \rightarrow s \models t \vee p$$

can be false: Given the truth-table for the inclusive disjunction it follows that the disjunction is only false in case both disjuncts t and p are false. This means that one can move to a direct attempt for a counterexample to show that there is a situation in which the conclusion is false and yet the premises true rendering, by definition, the argument invalid. This is much faster than the cumbersome procedure of performing the exhaustive search using a full truth-table. The construction of what one may characterize as the 'short' truth-table follows the method:

1. *The conclusion is forced false (1):*

$$p \vee q \quad q \rightarrow \neg s \quad \neg t \rightarrow s \models t \vee p$$
$$\;\bot$$
$$\;1$$

2. *In accordance with the truth-table for the disjunction this means that t is false (2).*

3. *It also means that p is false for the same reason (3).*

4. *From here the truth-values from the conclusion of the right-hand side of the semantic turnstile may be distributed to the premises on the left-hand side first with respect to p (4).*

5. *Then with respect to t (5).*

6. *That is not enough to go on since only p and t are assigned truth-values. We would like to force the premises true which for the first premise's part, $p \vee q$, means that the disjunction should be true (6).*

7. *Since p is false, but $p \vee q$ should be true, q must be true (7).*

8. *Similarly, the second premise $q \rightarrow \neg s$ should also be forced true (8).*

$$\begin{array}{ccccccccccc}
p & \vee & q & q & \rightarrow & \neg s & \neg & t & \rightarrow & s \models t & \vee & p \\
\bot & \top & \top & & \top & & & \bot & & & \bot & \bot & \bot \\
4 & 6 & 7 & & 8 & & & 5 & & & 2 & 1 & 3
\end{array}$$

9. *From item 7 it is known that q must be true (9).*

10. *If the antecedent q is true and we are attempting to make the whole implication $q \rightarrow \neg s$ true, then $\neg s$ should be true (10).*

11. *Since $\neg s$ should be true, s must be false (11).*

12. *Now take a look at the last premise $\neg t \rightarrow s$. An attempt to force it true will fail since we know from item 5 that t is false (12).*

13. *From item 11 it is known that s is false (13).*

14. *Since t is false, $\neg t$ must be true. The antecedent in $\neg t \rightarrow s$ is therefore true but the consequent false, which makes it impossible to force $\neg t \rightarrow s$ true (14):*

3. Validities

p	$\vee$	q	q	$\to$	$\neg$	s	$\neg$	t	$\to$	s	$\models$	t	$\vee$	p
$\bot$	T	T	T	T	T	$\bot$		$\bot$	T	$\bot$		$\bot$	$\bot$	$\bot$
4	6	7	9	8	10	11	14	5	12	13		2	1	3

↑ (under 14)

It is not possible to find a situation in which the premises are true but the conclusion false. The semantical consequence is once again demonstrated valid.

3.3 Connectives, Paths and Trees

The truth-tables for the logical connectives may be represented graphically in special *trees*. Consider by way of example the statement $A \wedge B$. This formula is true if both A and B are true. One may accordingly place A and B on a path leading from $A \wedge B$ (figure 3.1).

FIGURE 3.1. The path for $A \wedge B$.

Consider conversely $A \vee B$. This statement is true if either A is true or B is true. Thus there are two possibilities for making $A \vee B$ true. One may therefore position A and B under $A \vee B$ on separate paths in accordance with figure 3.2.

FIGURE 3.2. The paths for $A \vee B$.

The rules for 'branching' connectives in trees like these are called *tableaux rules*. These tableaux rules may be used as means for graphical representations of 'short truth-tables'.

3.3.1 Negation

The negation has only one rule. After the rule has been applied a '✓' is placed to indicate that the operation has been carried out for the particular statement in question.

Negation

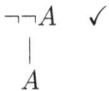

The rule for negation just says that *not-not-A* is logically equivalent to A.

3.3.2 Conjunction

The remaining connectives have two tableaux rules: One for the connective and one for its negation. The latter rule amounts to saying that the statement in which the conjunction serves as the main connective is false, or that the negated statement in which the conjunction is the main connective is true. Similarly for the other connectives.

A conjunction is true exactly when both conjuncts are true. A conjunction is false if either the first conjunct or the second conjunct or both conjuncts are false. This explains the two separate paths leading from $\neg(A \wedge B)$ in the $\neg\wedge$-rule.

3.3.3 Disjunction

The inclusive disjunction is true when either one or the other disjunct or both disjuncts are true. Conversely, the disjunction is only false when both disjuncts are false:

34   3. Validities

Disjunction

∨-rule

$A \vee B$ ✓
   /\
$A \quad B$

¬∨-rule

$\neg(A \vee B)$ ✓
  |
$\neg A$
$\neg B$

3.3.4 *Material implication*

The material implication is true either when the consequent is true or the antecedent false. The implication is false exactly when the antecedent is true and the consequent false.

Material implication

→-rule

$A \rightarrow B$ ✓
  /\
$\neg A \quad B$

¬→-rule

$\neg(A \rightarrow B)$ ✓
  |
A
$\neg B$

3.3.5 *Bi-implication*

The bi-implication is true when both the antecedent and consequent are true and when both of them are false. On the other hand, the bi-implication is only false in those cases where the antecedent is true but the consequent false or vice versa:

Bi-implication

↔-rule

$A \leftrightarrow B$ ✓
  /\
$A \quad \neg A$
$B \quad \neg B$

¬↔-rule

$\neg(A \leftrightarrow B)$ ✓
  /\
$A \quad \neg A$
$\neg B \quad B$

The intimate connection between the tableaux-rules and the truth-tables for the connectives may be depicted in the following way:

$$(\top\neg)\quad\begin{array}{c}\neg A\\\top\\|\\A\\\bot\end{array}\qquad\begin{array}{c}\neg A\\\bot\\|\\A\\\top\end{array}\quad(\bot\neg)$$

$$(\top\wedge)\quad\begin{array}{c}A\wedge B\\\top\\|\\A,\ B\\\top\ \top\end{array}\qquad\begin{array}{c}A\wedge B\\\bot\\\diagup\diagdown\\A\quad B\\\top\quad\bot\end{array}\quad(\bot\wedge)$$

$$(\top\vee)\quad\begin{array}{c}A\vee B\\\top\\\diagup\diagdown\\A\quad B\\\top\quad\top\end{array}\qquad\begin{array}{c}A\vee B\\\bot\\|\\A,\ B\\\bot\ \bot\end{array}\quad(\bot\vee)$$

$$(\top\to)\quad\begin{array}{c}A\to B\\\top\\\diagup\diagdown\\A\quad B\\\bot\quad\top\end{array}\qquad\begin{array}{c}A\to B\\\bot\\|\\A,\ B\\\top\ \bot\end{array}\quad(\bot\to)$$

$$(\top\leftrightarrow)\quad\begin{array}{c}A\leftrightarrow B\\\top\\\diagup\diagdown\\A,B\quad A,B\\\top\top\quad\bot\bot\end{array}\qquad\begin{array}{c}A\leftrightarrow B\\\bot\\\diagup\diagdown\\A,B\quad A,B\\\top\bot\quad\bot\top\end{array}\quad(\bot\leftrightarrow)$$

3.4 Semantic Tableaux

Consider the statement

$$((p \wedge q) \vee r) \wedge (s \to \neg r). \tag{3.4}$$

Using a tree it is possible to determine the conditions under which this statement is true—note that (3.4) is not a semantical consequence, just a statement. First attend to the main connective, which, given the parentheses is ∧. Then apply the ∧-rule:

36   3. Validities

$$((p \wedge q) \vee r) \wedge (s \rightarrow \neg r) \quad \checkmark$$
$$(p \wedge q) \vee r$$
$$s \rightarrow \neg r$$

Now the $\rightarrow$-rule is applied to $s \rightarrow \neg r$ which yields:

$$((p \wedge q) \vee r) \wedge (s \rightarrow \neg r) \quad \checkmark$$
$$(p \wedge q) \vee r$$
$$s \rightarrow \neg r \quad \checkmark$$
$$\diagup \quad \diagdown$$
$$\neg s \qquad \neg r$$

Apply the $\vee$-rule to $(p \wedge q) \vee r$ obtaining:

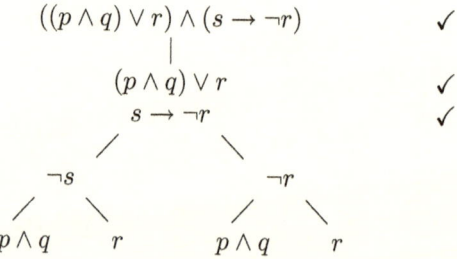

The two paths that stem from applying the $\vee$-rule must of course be placed from the node $\neg s$ as well as from the node $\neg r$. Finally apply the $\wedge$-rule to $p \wedge q$ at both nodes where $p \wedge q$ figures yielding the complete tree:

$$((p \wedge q) \vee r) \wedge (s \rightarrow \neg r) \quad \checkmark$$
$$(p \wedge q) \vee r \quad \checkmark$$
$$(s \rightarrow \neg r) \quad \checkmark$$
$$\diagup \qquad \diagdown$$
$$\neg s \qquad\qquad \neg r$$
$$\diagup\,\diagdown \qquad\qquad \diagup\,\diagdown$$
$$(p \wedge q) \; \checkmark \quad r \qquad (p \wedge q) \; \checkmark \quad r$$
$$\qquad\qquad p \qquad \uparrow \qquad\qquad p \qquad \times$$
$$\qquad\qquad q \qquad \varphi_2 \qquad\qquad q$$
$$\qquad\qquad \uparrow \qquad\qquad\qquad \uparrow$$
$$\qquad\qquad \varphi_1 \qquad\qquad\qquad \varphi_3$$

There are no more statements to decompose. Every complex statement has been decomposed into atomic statements (or their negations). One of the paths includes both r and $\neg r$. It is accordingly not possible to make all the statements in this path true simultaneously. The path is *closed*, and this is indicated by '×'. The remaining paths do not include an atomic statement and its negation which means that all the statements in each and every one of these paths can be made true simultaneously. They are called *open* paths.

Every open path gives rise to a partial truth ascription φ.[1] For example there is a partial truth ascription φ_1 such that:

$$\varphi_1 \quad \begin{array}{ccc} p & q & s \\ \downarrow & \downarrow & \downarrow \\ \top & \top & \bot \end{array}$$

Similarly φ_2 and φ_3 are produced by the following truth-value assignments:

$$\varphi_2 \quad \begin{array}{cc} r & s \\ \downarrow & \downarrow \\ \top & \bot \end{array} \qquad \varphi_3 \quad \begin{array}{ccc} p & q & r \\ \downarrow & \downarrow & \downarrow \\ \top & \top & \bot \end{array}$$

These trees are also called *semantic tableaux*.

3.5 Checking Trees

Semantic tableaux may be used as a procedure to check the validity of arguments. Once again in accordance with the fundamental definition of validity (7) a semantical consequence is valid if it is impossible to describe a situation in which the premises are true but the conclusion false. Given this definition we attempt to find exactly such a situation by constructing the counterexample depicted in figure 3.3 putting the procedure on par with the one described for the 'short' truth-tables.

The tableaux rules are then deployed for the logical connectives to the premises and the negation of the conclusion and checked off with '✓' one by one as we go through the statements to see whether the counterexample is consistent or inconsistent. The

---

[1] All open paths of a given tree accordingly provide the complete truth ascription since atomic statements which do not occur in the branch may be ascribed arbitrary truth-values.

38   3. Validities

FIGURE 3.3. The construction of the counterexample set in semantic tableaux.

counterexample set is *consistent* if it is possible to describe a situation in which the premises are true but the conclusion false, i.e. there exists at least one open path in the tableaux.

The semantical consequence is invalid if the counterexample set is consistent.

The counterexample set is conversely *inconsistent* if it is not possible to find such open paths and consequently the semantical consequence is valid and we can once again write $A_1, \ldots, A_n \models K$.

The semantical consequence is valid, if the counterexample set is inconsistent.

Consider the semantical consequence

$$p \wedge q, \neg(\neg q \vee r), \neg r \to \neg p \models (p \to \neg q) \qquad (3.5)$$

and do a semantic tableaux by constructing the counterexample set and checking it for consistency:

3. Validities   39

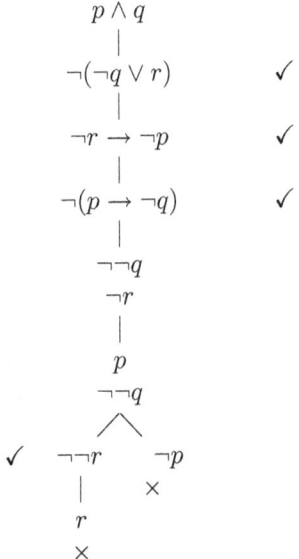

The semantic tableaux reveals that there are no open paths:

The counterexample set under which the premises are true and the conclusion false is inconsistent and therefore the semantical consequence is valid.

The construction of semantic tableaux is, like the application of truth-tables, completely mechanical. It is simply a matter of knowing the tableaux rules for the logical connectives and then combining systematically. Even though the tableaux method is significantly more efficient in checking for validity than the truth-tables they can still get fairly big if there are many statements involved in the argument. It is an advantage to develop the semantic tableaux in accordance with the following heuristics:

1. *First apply the tableaux rules to the statements which have $\wedge, \neg\vee$ and $\neg\rightarrow$ as the main connective since they only occasion one path.*

2. *Then apply the tableaux rules to the statements which have $\neg\wedge, \vee, \rightarrow, \leftrightarrow, \neg\leftrightarrow$ as the main connective since they occasion two paths.*

There is much more to be said about validity, semantic tableaux, methods of logic and their relations to science and society but for now, follow Tom Hanks as *Forrest Gump* when he says:

That's all I have to say about that!

4
Fallacies

I killed my logic teacher when I was 16. Allegedly self-defense – and what defense would be more legitimate? – I managed to be absolved by five votes against two, and I went to live under a bridge of the Seine, though I have never been in Paris.

—Campos de Carvalho

There is a catalogue of argument formats which are misleading and deceptive and have nothing to do with validity nor subject matter for that matter. Their power to install a conviction in those who hear them is tied to a motivation very different from not ending up as an intellectual vegetable. As compelling as they may seem, such arguments are fallacious from a logical point of view, and they are in turn referred to as *fallacies*.

4.1 Jump

So far there is only one way of jumping from the premises to the conclusion and that is via '$\therefore$' and the validity of the argument.

$$\left.\begin{array}{rl} 1. & A_1 \\ 2. & A_2 \\ 3. & A_3 \\ & \vdots \\ n. & A_n \\ \text{validity} & \end{array}\right\} \quad \therefore \quad K$$

Once the premises of an argument are accepted, then one is forced to accept the conclusion if the argument is valid. The force to accept the conclusion is cashed out in the prospects of contradicting oneself if one refrains.

Every day arguments may fall short of validity but they can all the same still induce convictions, change opinions, divide or dodge decisions, and alter actions. The jump from the car salesman's hard sales' talk to your decision to buy new wheels may be based on everything from his 'expert' opinion to feeling pity for him if you don't buy the product he is selling because he is ready out of business otherwise.

$$\begin{aligned} &1. \quad A_1 \\ &2. \quad A_2 \\ &3. \quad A_3 \\ &\quad \vdots \\ &n. \quad A_n \end{aligned}$$

$$\left. \begin{array}{l} \text{force} \\ \text{popularity} \\ \text{pity} \\ \text{authority} \\ \ldots \end{array} \right\} \curvearrowright \quad K$$

There are numerous jumps '$\curvearrowright$' from premises $A_1, A_2, A_3, ..., A_n$ to conclusion K other than the valid jump. The ability to recognize misleading and deceptive arguments, fallacies, may render them ineffective and powerless in debate, dispute, and disagreement. Some fallacies are easier to identify than others because the logical error committed is immediate. The argument schema

1. $A \to B$
2. B
3. $\therefore A$

is invalid since it ignores the possibility that there are other conditions apart from A that may lead to B. Suppose it is true that 'If there is financial inequality between the US and Mexico, then the two nations will go to war' and it also true that the two countries will go to war, then the fallacy of *affirming the consequent* is committed if it is concluded on the basis of them going to war that there is financial inequality between the US and Mexico. The two countries may go to war for a number of reasons not associated with financial inequalities like the drug trafficking problem across the border around El Paso or political differences.

A similar fallacy is known as *denying the antecedent:*

1. $A \to B$

2. $\neg A$

3. $\therefore \neg B$

The schema is invalid for the same reason as affirming the antecedent since some alternative explanation or cause is overlooked. Just because A is false there may be other conditions sufficing for making B true.

Knowing fallacies to be invalid and self-serving – and being knowledgeable of the structural reasons for their invalidity – one may isolate the strategies for inducing convictions and changing opinions and guard against being forced into believing anything for other reasons than the logical one. Below are some of the most notorious fallacies known since Antiquity which also explains their Latin labels.

4.2 Brute Force

The Russian-American philosopher, Ayn Rand, once said:

> There are only two means by which men can deal with one another: guns or logic. Force or persuasion. Those who know that they cannot win by means of logic, have always resorted to guns.

Ad Baculum arguments appeal to force or fear or both. When someone threatens,

$$\text{You'll do it or else ...} \tag{4.1}$$

and is ready to put his money where his mouth is, he is applying a brute force argument. Compliance is not dependent upon whether it is the best thing to do, or whether the induced conviction is logically deduced, but on what will happen to the opponent failing to comply. The argumentative power is given by the fact that the consequences are real and may happen. In a lovers quarrel, the argument is often unspoken but the threat to withdraw love may be real enough all the time. Similarly, a landlord saying,

$$\text{No pets allowed} \tag{4.2}$$

and the consequences are eviction, or threatening with extortion or blackmail and the consequences of exposure and/or prosecution, are all other instances of arguments appealing to feelings of fear or the use of force.

Being on the horns of the dilemma when someone has resorted to guns a choice must often be made between the cost of complying and the cost of denying. In the McCarthy Senate Hearings in the 1950's, all those summoned to testify before the committee, guilty and innocent as well, were forced to implicate and incriminate their friends and acquaintances or be labeled as involved in Communist insurrection and subsequently blacklisted.

Ad Baculum arguments are also used in less dramatic scenarios in advertising and sales campaigns. However morbid, signs like

$$\text{How will your family pay the bills?} \qquad (4.3)$$

while trying to sell life insurances, or 'How will you pay the bills?' as an argument for selling hospital insurances are typical tools of persuasion. A similar slogan like

$$\text{When the crash comes you will lose all your savings if you haven't had my expert advice!} \qquad (4.4)$$

may be used by an 'expert' trying to sell everything from cemetery plots, smoke alarms, fire extinguishers, protective devices from pepper sprays over prophylactics to the bigger air bags. Fear of loss is used by direct mail promotions that raises recipient's hopes with promises of valuable information if they only pay a small fee.[1] If the fee is not paid, the consequence is dire loss in some measure. Interestingly enough, the possible gain is often specified in immaculate detail, the loss in, say, direct mail ads is left obscure, perhaps because the product is obscure and was never needed in the first place.

4.3 The Man

Ad Hominem arguments are directed at the person rather than the subject matter in a given exchange of opinion. The idea, often as a last resort, is to launch a personal attack on the person who presents or endorses a certain viewpoint. Poisoning the well, an

---

[1] Information that in turn will cut taxes, save money, make money in sweepstakes and lotteries, offer psychic help which will bring even more money, offer good luck and love, etc.

ad hominem argument is designed to destroy the credibility of the person holding the point of view in question and destroy his argument accordingly. Such a strategy is extensively applied to discredit candidates for election by trick-campaigns that reveal irrelevant facts about a candidate's private life to the public.

By way of example, in the 1992 election, Ross Perot was in the eye of the political tornado, not so much for what he was saying politically, but rather because of his manner, attitude, walk and voice, his big ears and his negligible size to some. In the TV-duel between Al Gore and Perot, the US administration admitted that they had launched an attempt to influence the vote toward the North American Free Trade Agreement (NAFTA) from 1992 by making its opponents appear ridiculous. The news media are also generally expected to provide the public with unbiased reporting but during elections voters are witnesses to derogatory adjectives and direct personal attacks on candidates from one or the other side depending on what TV-station one happens to be watching.

Ad hominem arguments have some close allies one of them being the *guilt by association* argument. When the girlfriend says

$$\text{You sound just like your mother!} \quad (4.5)$$

and your mother is considered unpopular, the attack is launched in the hope of making your stance unpopular just because your mother is. When someone says in response to your point of view

$$\text{That sounds like something the Democrats would say ...} \quad (4.6)$$

the tacit strategy is to get you first to agree to the allegedly ridiculous nature of some Democratic view and then launch an attack undermining your credibility by pointing to the ridiculous Democratic cause you just happened to endorse. A political commentator once attempted to join Elizabeth Dole with Hillary Rodham Clinton in the minds of voters by pointing to similarities in their background and education.

A final ally to the *ad hominem* is the *tu quoque*-construction or the 'you, too'-argument. In essence this is the

$$\text{Practice what you preach,} \quad (4.7)$$

or two wrongs make a right argument;

$$\text{If you can do it, so can I} \quad (4.8)$$

which is just what you might find between you and your lover in the sense that

$$\text{Sauce for the goose is sauce for the gander.} \qquad (4.9)$$

4.4 Authority

Arguments based on appeals to authority are called *Ad Verecundiam* arguments. With varying success children are trained not to dispute their parents and elders which constitute the authorities in their lives, and that training continues to condition adults to follow authorities often with little or no dispute. In turn, and like parents, employers are considered authorities because of their immediate power over employees; and government is taken to be an authority because of its power over the people of a nation. In personal disputes, one contender will assault the other's opinions by claiming to be or quoting someone taken to be an authority.

Genuine authorities are hard to come by and the practice to doubt an authority is also part of the arguing game. In trials of crime it is not too uncommon for both the defense and prosecution to present expert witnesses who in turn voice completely opposite opinions. Doctors are often considered as being authorities and commercials rely heavily on this conception in 'More doctors prescribe ...,' 'More hospitals use ...,' 'More dentists advise ....' Endorsements by movie stars, sports figures, models and the like serve the same ends and imply both that they are authorities and that their saying so makes 'this' *the* thing to do or *the* product to purchase.

4.5 The Masses

Ad Populum arguments are appeals to the people or the masses' opinion or viewpoint. The appeal is in essence the need to belong to or to be accepted within some group or community. Liking what most like must be good,

$$\text{1.000.000 Elvis fans can't be wrong,} \qquad (4.10)$$

doing what most people do must be right, even truth may sometimes be settled by a majority vote. Even if it stands to determine what most people fancy in one way or the other – which may be hard enough in itself – what most people like, do or even believe, does not settle taste, moral sentiment or truth.

That aside, the great anonymous 'everybody' exerts substantial social pressure to conform. At election time, when one person is ahead in the polls, that will often be enough to swing voters in the direction favorable to the candidate. Voters persuaded to vote the Democratic ticket since 'they' are for the 'the blue-collar workers,' to vote the Republican ticket because 'they' are for the 'the white-collar people' results from an argument of this nature. From time to time, members of Congress are pressured to vote for their party lines and from time to time members of religious, ethnic and racial groups support their leaders simply because they are members of the given group.

Not only do some arguments appeal to the masses but also to tradition—sacred cows. This argument, a close kin to *ad populum* arguments, appeal to those ideas, ideals and principles that people claim to respect; say, loyalty and friendship, patriotism, rights and freedom, profit and capitalism, fair division and socialism, and the democratic form of government, etc. To challenge or disagree implies that one is against, not the argument *per se*, but what the majority holds dear.

4.6 Ignorance

Ad Ignorantiam arguments rely on ignorance. Suppose something cannot be demonstrated wrong (in the evaluative sense), then it must be right in this sense. One may view both opponents and proponents of the aforementioned NAFTA-disagreement as users of this argument; the treaty was good/bad for the US because it could not be demonstrated otherwise.

4.7 Begging it

The structure of an argument begging the question, also known as *petito principii*, is *circularity*: The argument assumes what it tries to prove, so the conclusion to be reached is really the premise started out with. The way in which the Bush Administration argued for Iraq hiding weapons was begging the very question the UN inspectors were trying to prove. Another *petito principii* argument is one for the existence of God in which God caused the

Bible to be written and the Bible says there is God. A similar circular theological argument is to be found in the Koran used to prove the existence of Allah. Arguments on empty premises may beg the circularity issue too like tautologies of the form 'women are female' or 'men are male.'

4.8 Claim, Data and Warrant

Above is but a small sample of the most common fallacies—there are more and the reason is roughly this: If validity is not the reason for accepting the conclusion of an argument, then what is? There may be infinitely many reasons for siding with one point of view or the other – one for every non-deductive conclusion endorsed – so search for validity first and infinity later.

In search for argument structure the following general model of argumentation provided by the American philosopher Stephen Toulmin, and sometimes referred to as *Toulmin's model*, is often useful:

$$D \longrightarrow A$$
$$\mid$$
$$W$$

According to the model, argumentation consists of three parts:

- A: The *claim* that is being argued.
- D: The *data* which provides support for the claim.
- W: The *warrant* which establishes the (often implicit) connection between the claim and the data. A warrant may be a general rule which licences the move from D to A.

Here is one of Toulmin's own examples to demonstrate the way in which the model works:

Do you have a point to make?
 Claim: Harry is a British subject.
What do you have to go on?
 Data: Harry was born in Bermuda.
What is to be believed for the data to support the claim?
 Warrant: Anyone born in Bermuda is a British subject.

5

Modalities

I know what I believe. I will continue to articulate what I believe and what I believe. I believe what I believe is right.
—George W. Bush Jr.

Since the beginning, a guiding principle has been that every statement is either true or false. Truth-conditions then specify in what situations statements are true or false. The truth-conditional characteristics for some statements is easy to lay down, take the useless contradictions and the equally uninformative tautologies by way of example—one is never true, the other always true. Contingent statements and their truth-conditional characteristics are sometimes straight-forward as well but the closer the move to the idioms and statements of natural language, the harder the semantical behavior gets to handle and account for. Some statements of natural language almost run wild semantically. Sometimes the semantics for natural language statements is so tough to account for – despite their continuous usage – that thought and talk perhaps would be much better off without them on many occasions.

5.1 Intensions

Besides the principle of bivalence, another principle has tacitly been in play all along:

Definition 9 The Principle of Extensionality: *The truth-value of a statement A depends solely on the actual situation.*

The classical logic used in the previous chapters obeys the principle of extensionality. That is the reason why it has earned its name *classical*. The statement

$$\text{Imelda Marcos is beyond logic and rationality} \quad (5.1)$$

is taken to be a declarative statement either true or false of the actual circumstances or situation. Similarly, the statement

Depicting sacred figures in a ludicrous way insults people (5.2)

is also true or false of the actual situation—either the statement describes a state of affairs in which people are offended by caricatures or it does not. If it does, the statement is true, otherwise it is false of the actual situation. Unsure whether Imelda Marcos is beyond logic and rationality someone might say

It is possible that Imelda Marcos
is beyond logic and rationality. (5.3)

while being sure that obscene depictions are insulting someone might utter

It is necessary that depicting sacred figures
in a ludicrous way insults people. (5.4)

Let '$\Diamond$' stand for 'It is possible that ...', and let '$\Box$' denote 'It is necessary that ...' and recast statements (5.3) and (5.4) as respectively

$$\Diamond A \quad \text{and} \quad \Box B,$$

where A represents (5.1) and B presents (5.2).

$\Diamond$ are $\Box$ also connectives, called *operators*, working on well-formed statements but they are not classical connectives in the extensional sense. While A and B are either true or false of the actual situation it is not immediately clear how the truth-conditions for $\Diamond A$ and $\Box B$ should be determined. One could try to proceed in the traditional fashion with truth-tables:

A	$\Diamond A$
$\top$	$\top$
$\bot$	?

1

B	$\Box B$
$\top$	?
$\bot$	$\bot$

2

If A is true, A is also trivially possible; if B is in fact false, then B can't be necessary true. On the other hand, just because A actually is false, so Imelda Marcos is not beyond logic and rationality, this does not say anything about whether A is possible, that is, whether there still exists a situation in which Imelda Marcos transcends logic and rationality. Similarly, if B is true of the actual situation this does not suffice for determining whether B is necessarily so. Hence the ascription of truth-values for $\Diamond A$ and $\Box B$ is *underdetermined* given the actual situation. Possibility and necessity refer to ways in which statements are true or false—that is, other ways than the real way, or other situations than the actual one. Statements which are true or false relative to other situations than the actual situation are called *modalities*. $\Diamond$ and $\Box$ are also called *alethic* modalities, derived from 'alethia' which is the Latin word for truth.

Imelda Marcos, Former Minister of Human Settlements and Former Governor of Metro Manila is most likely not actually beyond logic and rationality even counting her 3000 pairs of shoes and bullet-proof bra. So one may simultaneously and without contradiction claim that

> *Imelda Marcos is not beyond logic and rationality, but the possibility is obviously still there.*

Thus, A is false, whereas $\Diamond A$ is true. One may argue for the truth of $\Diamond A$ in the actual situation if a situation is describable or imaginable where A is true, even though A is in fact false. Now let $w, v, u, \ldots$ denote arbitrary situations and let w be the actual situation. The considerations above suggest the following criterion for the truth of $\Diamond A$ in the actual world w:

  i. $\Diamond A$ *is true in w insofar there exists a situation v, accessible from w, in which A is true.*

Similarly for (5.4). If it is necessarily so that depicting sacred figures insults people, then there exists no situations in which obscene depictions of the sacred do not lead to insult, or put differently, in all possible situations it is the case that obscene depictions of the sacred are insulting to people. This consideration paves the way for the following criterion for the truth of $\Box B$ in the actual situation w:

  ii. $\Box B$ *is true in w, if for all other situations v, accessible from w, B is true in v.*

Truth-conditions for statements governed by possibility and necessity are indeed specifiable, but in order to do so the principle of extensionality ceases to hold. To determine the truth-conditions for modal statements of the above nature other possible situations besides the actual must be consulted. The modal statements and the arguments in which they figure require what is called *intensional* semantics, that is, semantics which take into account other possible states of affairs *accessible* or *inaccessible* for that matter from the actual state of affairs.

There are many modalities in natural language besides possibility and necessity: temporal modalities like 'in the future it will be the case that ...', deontic modalities like 'you are obligated to do ...', or 'you are permitted to do ...', epistemic modalities like 'I'm convinced that ...' and so on. Equally many modal logics have been developed attempting to come to terms with these terms. These logics are for another time. For now attention is confined to looking at two other types of modal expressions which in the current scheme of things, are particularly pertinent to thought and talk.

5.2 Counterfactuals

Hypothetical reasoning is a trademark of human thought. For instance, the American activist and writer Rita Mae Brown once said:

$$\text{If the world were a logical place,} \\ \text{men would ride side-saddle.} \tag{5.5}$$

On the surface the statement looks like an ordinary 'if ... then ...'-construction, and classically this is handled by the material implication. The material implication has definite truth-value ascriptions in the actual situation, so no mystery here. The trouble is the word 'were' figuring in the antecedent-condition. It indicates a hypothetical situation rather than an actual one which means that the antecedent does not necessarily have a truth-value ascription but rather a '?' like the ones for the truth-tables $\Diamond A$ and $\Box B$ above. Given 'were' (5.5) does not say that the world is a logical place, nor does it say that it couldn't be, so the antecedent simply fails to have a truth-value on the classical conception. A statement like (5.5) is known as a *counterfactual conditional* as it speaks of situations other than, or counter to, the actual situation.

Despite the fact that counterfactual conditionals are used all the time this does not make their semantic behavior any easier to account for. So the question still stands of how to provide truth-conditions for counterfactuals. The standard intensional semantics interprets counterfactuals accordingly: A counterfactual conditional, symbolized by

$$A \mapsto B$$

for arbitrary statements A and B, is true in the actual situation, insofar, in all those situations in which A is true that are in proximity 'closest' to the actual situation, B is also true in these 'closest' situations. More specifically of three situations w, w', w'' if w' is closer to w than w'', then $A \mapsto B$ will be true in w iff A is not true in any situation or there exist a situation w' in which A and B are true which is closer to w than any situation w'' in which A is true but B is false.

An example is in order explaining this business of closeness and proximity: Consider the counterfactual

If George W. Bush Jr. were not President of the US, then he would be Chairman of the NRA. (5.6)

This seems like a pretty plausible counterfactual statement. The reason is that the truth-conditions for (5.6) are not that hard to picture here and now in the actual situation. Just imagine a situation identical to the actual one save for the fact that George W. Bush Jr. is no longer President of the United States. If he in this hypothetical situation is Chairman of the National Riffle Association (which given his general inclinations and views of the world is at least possible) and there are no situations closer where he is not, then it is true in the actual situation here and now that 'If George W. Bush Jr. were not President of the US, then he would be Chairman of the NRA.'

Similarly

If I were not lecturing in this class, I would be modelling, (5.7)

is a less plausible counterfactual conditional unfortunately. In the closest situation to the actual one in which I'm not lecturing in this class, is one where I still look the way I do now. Twenty years ago the agency did not want me as a model—at least not for very long. Now, twenty years down the line show and I don't look the same, but worse, so the closest situation to the actual situation where I'm not lecturing is still a situation where the agency wouldn't want me. No Helena Christensen or Giselle Bundchen life for me, although 'If I were Helena Christensen or Giselle Bundchen, I would be modelling' is a different counterfactual even further out because imagining a situation in which I'm not lecturing is right at hand, getting to a situation in which I'm a Caucasian female with the right looks, that's a bit trickier.

The condition of accessibility from before, and here closeness or proximity, are troublesome notions in intensional semantics. They all hinge in one way or the other on a notion of *similarity* between situations. The more similar one situation is to another, the closer it is. Usually similarity is cashed out in terms of *ceteris paribus* clauses—everything-else-being-equal clauses: The less tinkering with a situation, everything else being equal, the more similar that situation is and accordingly the closer it is to the actual situation. From this perspective, floating around in a tank on a planet called Alpha Centauri or being victim of the *Matrix* on a daily basis, requires *ceteris paribus* more conditions to be changed than the situation in which you were born in Copenhagen rather than New York City. By all means use counterfactuals in thought to talk but be sure to stay close.

As for Rita Mae Brown, the situation in which the world is a logical place is way out there—sorry to say. Sorry for Rita Mae Brown and the male genitalia.

5.3 Attitudes

Between lovers, say, α and β one could easily imagine the following exchange taking place:

α: 'You didn't pick up the stuff from the pharmacy I told you to.'

β: 'I'm certain that I did.'

α: 'I know you didn't because I checked everywhere and it is nowhere in sight.'

β: 'Well, I guess I didn't then, if what you say is true.'

α: 'I know, so it is *the* truth. Why are you lying?'

β: 'I'm not lying, I just believe that I did pick it up, that's all.'

α: 'Believing doesn't make it so, you know!'

β: 'I'm aware of that, thank you!'

α: 'So why didn't you pick it up—you know how important it is.'

β: 'I wish I had picked it up ...'

α: 'Don't give me attitude and don't you patronize me. You don't understand. You don't understand me!'

β: 'Of course I understand you!'

α: 'I *feel* you don't understand me.'

β: 'Oh uh.'

α: 'Enough already, ... nothing for you tonight, I'm going to bed.'

β: 'I think I feel neglected ...'

All of 'know', 'certain', 'believe', 'aware', 'wish', 'understand' and 'feel' of this dispute are modal operators similar to $\lozenge$ and $\square$ yet different. Whereas necessity and possibility relate to the ways the world might be, 'know', 'certain', 'believe', 'aware', 'wish', 'understand' and 'feel' relate to a person and the attitude with respect to which the person in question takes a statement A to be true. 'I know that A,' 'I believe that A,' 'I'm aware that A,' 'I wish that A', ..., are called *propositional attitudes* as they express somebody's mood with respect to the way in which some statement A is considered true. To determine the truth-conditions for the statements involving propositional attitudes one is again forced to consult other situations than the actual situation.

For starters consider only knowledge and belief. Let α refer to a person and let

$$K_\alpha A \qquad (5.8)$$

be short-hand for 'α knows that A' while 'α believes that A' is symbolized by

$$B_\alpha C \qquad (5.9)$$

for arbitrary statements A and C. The classical truth-tables for (5.8) and (5.9) amount to the following:

A	$K_\alpha A$
$\top$	?
$\bot$	$\bot$

1

C	$B_\alpha C$
$\top$	?
$\bot$	?

2

Knowledge and belief give rise to even more question marks than possibility and necessity did. The only thing to be said for knowledge is that knowledge of A carries a requirement of truth of A. As a matter of definition it is a necessary but not sufficient condition for knowledge that whatever is known is also true. That is also the reason why α says 'I know, so it is *the* truth.' Truth alone is not sufficient for knowledge. It is true that 'verification-transcendent truth-conditions in intuitionistic logic are very complicated' but one may not know that, nor what verification-transcendent truth-conditions and intuitionistic logic are. Many things are true but a person might not know them; humans are not omniscient and that is the reason for the question mark, learning, education and you sitting here reading this text. However, the requirement of truth of A does ensure that if A is false, then so is $K_\alpha A$. 'Knowing something false' is by definition not knowledge but it may very well be belief. It is false that Einstein said 'Everything is relative', and it is also false that he got the Nobel Prize in Physics for the theory of relativity but someone – not saying who – might believe so anyway. Einstein became a Nobel Laureate in Physics for his theory of photo-electric effect but that does not entail that you believe or know this to be the case. So for $B_\alpha C$ there are question marks all over.

The standard intensional semantics for knowledge and belief introduces a partition of the set of situations into those that are compatible with the attitude in question and those that are incompatible with the attitude such that:

- $K_\alpha A$ *is true in w if for all other situations v compatible with what α knows, it is the case that A.*

- $B_\alpha C$ *is true in w if for all other situations v compatible with what α believes, it is the case that C.*

In fact, ascription of any propositional attitude requires a partition of the situations into those that are compatible and those incompatible with the attitude of interest. That goes for 'certain', 'believe', 'aware', 'wish', 'understand' and 'feel' too.

'Certain', 'believe', 'aware', 'wish', 'understand' and 'feel' are ranked between or below knowledge and belief. To be certain of something as β claims to be about picking up the stuff from the pharmacy is not the same as having knowledge of having picked up the goods. Where certainty is almost as strong as knowledge in terms of epistemic commitment, certainty does entail a margin of error, albeit small. This is the reason why β is bold enough to use this attitude, because also it leaves a way out if proven erroneous. When α then demonstrates knowledge of the fact that β did fail to bring home the goods, β's strategy is to weaken the commitment to belief instead. Belief is usually considered to have a higher margin of error than certainty which in turn has a higher margin of error than knowledge which again has none. Now, 'Believing doesn't make it so, you know' α shoots back, and so β is forced to admitting failing the pick-up and resorts to wishful thinking. Wishful thinking gets β into even more trouble because wishing is non-committal to truth but just expresses in this case a failed intention. Hell is now all loose because failing to put words into action in a non-logical way (unless some tacit premises are spelled out) now entails lack of understanding α. β's attempt to patch it up by claiming to understand α is a strategy dead in its tracks, because had he understood he would have picked up the contraceptives from the pharmacy which was the original subject-matter of the dispute. Only when α says 'I feel you don't understand me' does β realize this blunder but by that time it is all too late. In the end:

> β thinks he has been neglected since he didn't get any, and α feels the same way!

Knowledge, certainty, belief, awareness and possibly also understanding are all committed to truth in different degrees starting with knowledge and moving downwards from there. Besides the fact knowledge is on top of the scale due to its unequivocal commitment to the truth as a necessary condition by definition, where the other attitudes exactly lie on the epistemic scale is much debated in logic, epistemology, cognitive science and theoretical computer science.

On the other hand, 'β wishes that A' is not connected to the truth in any way, shape or form, wishing does not make it so. 'α feels that A' is at least as bad if not worse. Your feelings are indubitable, they do not stand a chance of refutation. 'I feel that ...' is true as long as you feel it regardless of what you feel something about and so you might as well just leave out the A—that would be the subject-matter! In a sense, statements of emotions are the strongest knock-down vehicles in any dispute as they are irrefutable, but they are also for this very reason the weakest vehicles of dispute. Tautologies are irrefutable as well as; they are always true and expressions of feelings are the same way as as long you have them. So statements of feelings are just as informative as uttering tautologies—information next to nothing. Feelings are fine, but they should just not enter into argument.

5.4 Opinions

When smut-peddler, founder and chief-editor of *Hustler Magazine*, Larry Flynt, was indicted for not revealing the source of a video tape allegedly showing FBI agents buying narcotics, the court addressed Flynt with the words 'It is the opinion of this court ...' to which Flynt immediately fired back:

> Well, opinions are like ass-holes your Honor—everybody's got one!

Of course this was way out of line by all means, but there is a line of reasoning to it which is sound enough. People are taught that their opinions are important; political, personal, profound. They sure are, but only when a valid argument useful for action, deliberation and decision can be presented in the favor of whatever opinion is finally settled upon. Remember what Former US-Senator, Ambassador and sociologist, Daniel P. Moynihan, said:

> You have the right to your own opinions but you do not have the right to your own facts.

Furthermore, adding modalities to statements when they are not required just obscures the semantics and makes the truth-conditions much harder to determine. If you can make do without them, do. Say what you have to say without the personal pronouns and the attitudes; if your argument is valid it will stand on its own. No additional strength is added by what is believed, felt, hoped or desired; a crisp, sound and valid argument—that is something to be admired.

6
Demonstrations

Logic will take you by the throat and force you to agree!

C.I. Lewis

An argument is a kind of proof or demonstration of a statement. There are templates of proof to use and different kinds of examples to cite in favor of, or to discredit, a statement.

6.1 Proofs

There are different formats for proving statements some of which have already been deployed during this crash course. They have only been implicitly described however. Proof procedures are deployed in daily thought and talk but are often implicit there too, albeit for different reasons. A few common proof strategies are reviewed explicitly below.

6.1.1 Proofs by Contradiction and Reductio ad Absurdum

In checking arguments as to their validity, truth-tables and semantic tableaux are methods of proof by *contradiction*. They have the following general structure. To prove $A \to C$ assume that A is true, and assume the truth of the negation of C too (this corresponds to establishing the counterexample set to the argument under investigation in the tableaux-methodology). From these facts it is deduced that A is false and hence the contradiction. The conclusion is in turn the truth of C. These lines of wordy explanation boils down to the simple fact that

$$(A \land \neg C) \to \neg A \qquad (6.1)$$

is logically equivalent to

$$A \to C \qquad (6.2)$$

and there is not much else to say about it.

A related proof-format is known as *reductio ad absurdum*. As before the goal is to establish $A \to C$. Suppose B is known to be a true statement. Set A to be true, and assume the negation of C to be true. Suppose it can now be demonstrated that these imply the truth of the negation of B, so B is false. Now B is both true and false which given the principle of bivalence is impossible. The conclusion is then that C is true.

6.1.2 Direct Proofs

The structure of a direct proof of a statement $A \to C$ is based on the *transitivity* of the material implication:

$$\text{If } A \to B \text{ and } B \to C, \text{ then } A \to C, \tag{6.3}$$

Assume that A is a true statement. From A, a statement, say A_1, is deduced, and from A_1 another statement A_2 is deduced and so it goes until this process yields $A_K \to C$. Since the material implication enjoys the transitivity property, $A \to C$ is in turn proved.

Although the idea of a direct proof is simple, almost too simple even, the trick is hidden in the status of the deduced statements $A_1, A_2, ..., A_k$. These deduced statements are themselves results obtained from other deductions, or introduced by definition. They are in effect statements known to be true. If these statements are known truths some of their consequences are known as well but there may be multiple derivable consequences.

By analogy, one may compare a direct proof to crossing a river using stepping stones. Standing on the river bank is knowing the statement A. Getting across the river is deducing the statement C. The stepping stones are in turn the intermediate statements each of which is a consequence of the other. Now, from each stone in the river, one may have the choice of several stones to reach next. The challenge is to decide which one is the best to use getting across and not somewhere else. The scenario from hell is of course to have no stones to go to because that will get you nowhere.

Many connections exist between statements but they are not all relevant in getting to C. Suppose it is known that x is a prime number. Here are some possible consequences of that thesis:

- The only positive divisors are 1 and x itself.

- If x is not 2, then it is an odd integer.

- If x is odd, then it is of the form $4k + 1$ or $4k - 1$ for some integer k.

Which one to pick is not only dependent on the final destination but also on the intermediate rest-stops and having knowledge of other results is crucial to the success of a direct proof.

If unsuccessful in solving a problem using a direct proof one may be tempted to work backwards to see how a solution may have looked. In a direct proof of a conditional statement $A \to C$, C is known. Caution should be exercised when working backwards with the answer assumed because the backwards process does not constitute a proof even if successful. If C is assumed and a true statement like '$1 = 1$' is deduced, then this does not license the conclusion that C is true. First of all, the alleged proof may never use the antecedent statement A—what has been proven so far is only that

$$C \to 1 = 1. \tag{6.4}$$

Secondly, the tautological statement '$1 = 1$' is true whenever C is true but also whenever C is false. Finally, what has been proved at best is that the converse statement is not equivalent to the original one. Think of 'if x is odd, then $2x$ is even' and the reason why $2x$ being even does not imply that x is odd.

6.1.3 Proofs by Induction

A proof by induction has not been encountered so far, but a definition by induction has. When the set of well-formed statements for the propositional language was described in chapter 2, page 18, induction was deployed. The set of well-formed statements described in that hidden definition may be expressed with much more elegance and precision in the following definition: Let a collection of propositional symbols be given as before. The set of well-formed statements may be defined as the *smallest* set X such that

(i) Every propositional symbol, **p**, is a well-formed statement.

(ii) If $A, B \in X$, then $\neg A \in X, A \wedge B, A \vee B, A \to B, A \leftrightarrow B \in X$.

A specification of the atomic statements is initially provided followed by a description of how the complex statements are constructed from the ones already given. (i) is called the *induction basis* or *induction hypothesis*, while (ii) is called the *induction step*.

In a proof based on induction one shows that an inductively defined set has a certain property by demonstrating that the elements of the induction basis have the property and that this property is maintained under induction. By way of example it is inductively provable that every well-formed statement of the propositional language has an even number of parentheses: An atomic statement has 0 parentheses. Suppose that A and B are well-formed statements which have $2n$ and $2m$ parentheses respectively. Then every one of $(A \land B), (A \lor B), (A \to B)$ and $(A \leftrightarrow B)$ have

$$2(n + m + 1)$$

parentheses. If A has $2n$ parentheses, then $\neg A$ has precisely $2n$ parentheses. Now, an atomic statement has 0 parentheses and 0 is even, and since the well-formed statements have to obey the conditions stated on page 18, the lowest number of parentheses in a complex statement is 2, and 2 is an even number too.

Proofs by induction pay homage to the idea that the next step in the proof process is licensed or legitimized by the former step as the American logician and philosopher Alan Ross Anderson once explained:

> All logic manuscripts contain infinitely many errors.
> Proof: For every error you find there is another one.

6.2 A Knowledge Primer

Often examples are also used for demonstration. Some examples are good, some are terrible. Here is an example about knowledge to illustrate examples.

Implicit in the work of Plato, later also endorsed by the German philosopher Immanuel Kant (1724–1807), and recently explicitly described by the American philosopher C.I. Lewis, knowledge is characterized by three individually necessary and jointly sufficient ingredients: Truth, belief and justification. The *standard tripartite analysis of knowledge* still largely entertained in epistemology (also called the theory of knowledge) pays tribute to the idea that person α knows a statement A insofar as the following conditions are met with satisfaction:

α knows A iff

1. α believes A,

2. *A is true*,

3. α *is justified in believing A*.

Believing is typically considered as being a psychological primitive or a dispositional psychological state. The state exists independently of manifestation. Belief has not raised any serious eyebrows as an ingredient of knowledge. This first condition is essentially a condition hooking up the person α to the statement A known. Knowledge presupposes belief that A but meeting condition 1 alone is not sufficient for knowledge of A. The belief that A may turn out false. Humans are free to believe something which is in fact false but knowledge is not such a lenient commitment as already discussed in the previous chapter. This paves the way for condition 2. The tripartite analysis accordingly suggests, as an additional necessary condition, that knowledge of A entails the truth of A.

A claim to knowledge requires that the meeting of the belief-condition 1 with the truth-condition 2 is 'adequate'. The two conditions 1 and 2 alone are jointly insufficient to pan out in knowledge. True beliefs may be the result of blind luck, clairvoyance, random guessing etc. Beliefs generated by such procedures should not amount to knowledge. The reason is the rather obscure and seemingly unreliable procedures or means by which the actually true beliefs have been produced. The adequate meeting is severed and condition 3 is instated. The condition is there to provide supportive reasons describing why the first two conditions are suitably connected. Only furnished with such supportive reasons together with the other two conditions may the person be said to have the necessary and sufficient testimony required for knowledge.

6.2.1 A Good Example

In a three page paper 'Is Knowledge Justified Belief?' from 1963 the American philosopher Edmund Gettier gave the now legendary and quite scandalous counterexamples to knowledge as true justified belief. The British philosopher and mathematician Bertrand Russell (1872–1970) had anticipated the counterexamples in the late 1940's:

> It is clear that knowledge is a subclass of true beliefs. [...] There is a man who looks at a clock when it is not going, though he thinks that it is, and who happens

to look at it at the moment when it is right; this man acquires a true belief as to the time of day, but cannot be said to have knowledge. There is the man who believes, truly, that the last name of the prime minister in 1906 began with a B, but who believes this because he thinks that Balfour was prime minister then, whereas in fact it was Campbell Bannerman.

Even a stopped clock gets the right time twice a day. Looking at it just in time does not suffice for knowing what time it is. Now Russell anticipated these problems, but the explicit formulation of the counterexamples are due to Gettier. The counterexamples have partly fixed the agenda for epistemological research since.

The Gettier-examples often involve the derivation of something true from something false. Smith may have in the past collected firm evidence which together with other relevant background information furnish supportive reasons for, or perhaps even deductively entail, the following statement about Jones' possessions with respect to automotive vehicles:

A_1: *Jones owns a Ford car*

Suppose Smith has an acquaintance, Brown. Smith does not know where Brown is. For no particular reason Smith uses his internal randomizer and chooses a location, say Boston, as Brown's current location. Then by applying the truth-table for the disjunction Smith concludes:

$$\text{Jones owns a Ford car} \lor \text{Brown is in Boston.} \qquad (6.5)$$

The fact that the two statements have nothing to do with each other does not matter for the truth of (6.5). Even if 'Brown is in Boston' is false 'Jones owns a Ford car' is supposedly true so the entire disjunction remains true. Now, if the derivation is valid for Boston, it will be valid for Barcelona and Brest-Litovsk as well. Smith constructs the following three disjunctive hypotheses immediately entailed by A_1:

A_2: *Jones owns a Ford car* $\lor$ *Brown is in Boston*

A_3: *Jones owns a Ford car* $\lor$ *Brown is in Barcelona*

A_4: *Jones owns a Ford car* $\lor$ *Brown is in Brest-Litovsk*

Let Smith accept A_2, A_3 and A_4 based on his solid belief in A_1. Given the standard tripartite definition of knowledge, Smith is then justified in his belief of A_2, A_3 and A_4. He is cleared to consider them as instances of knowledge. Odd, since by randomizing

Smith has no clue to Brown's whereabouts though that again does not matter for the disjunctive truth

Gettier then tells the story that Jones in fact drives a rented car from *AVIS* (or something like it) so it is not his own Ford. Brown however is by accident in Barcelona. This information is still not available to Smith. It follows nevertheless that Smith is justified in believing A_3 but he does not know that A_3 is true. Smith has gotten things right but for the wrong reasons: He claims to have knowledge because he apparently has reasons to believe that Jones owns a Ford, which he does not. All the same, truth is preserved because unknown to Smith, Brown is in fact in Barcelona. Smith's original reasons for believing and being justified are undercut. According to the standard definition of knowledge however Smith may still be accredited with knowledge.

Such Gettier-examples and more like them are at one and the same time both virulent and primitive diseases. They point to a fundamental flaw in the classical conception of knowledge and do so by using quite simple means like the truth-table for disjunction. A particularly malignant feature of the paradoxes is the fact that one may comfortably remain in the actual situation observing the Gettier-cases. Given the truth-conditions for the two disjuncts one may extensionally compute the truth-value for the entire disjunction. One is not required to invoke intensional measures and other possible situations besides the actual for this computation. In other words, Gettier-paradoxes do not require modal universes for their formulation—not much tampering with the situation to create the knowledge flaw.

That is what makes the Gettier-examples good examples. You stay in the actual situation or close to it. Solutions to the Gettier-paradoxes, however, most often rely on modal notions of knowledge. While the Gettier-problems are virulent but primitive, the cures are often modal and complex prescribing rather strong medicine.

6.2.2 A Bad Example

One often hears the characterization that philosophy is much about *conceptual analysis*. That goes in epistemology as well. The goal of these new conceptual exercises is to spell out and elucidate some of the significant notions like knowledge, justification and rationality that ordinary folk use on a daily basis. An integral part of the elucidation process is to stretch the usage of these concepts to the *max* in order to reveal their limitations and what these limits in turn reveal about the nature of human cognition. Seen from this perspective conceptual analysis is much about how words are used in everyday contexts.

The actual 'stretching' is performed by applying the method of 'consulting intuitions about possible cases' as the philosopher Frank Jackson recently made a case for. Jackson takes conceptual analysis to be an indispensable part of intellectual activity in general. Others restrict the conceptual analysis to philosophical concepts but the overall ambition is less modest: To argue for the authority and autonomy of philosophy where philosophy has a privileged subject matter only accessible by *a priori* methods; a subject matter which scientific method cannot even hope to reach.

The Gettier-example was a good counterexample of reasoning by examples. Here is another example relying heavily on conceptual analysis and the intuitions about possible cases which also underlies the Wachowski-brothers three *Matrix* movies. Since Plato it has been the standard opinion of philosophers and epistemologists that knowledge is, or should be, true and infallible. When I say that I know that I'm reading the newspaper now, it means that right now there are no reasonably imaginable circumstances in which I'm not reading the newspaper. Had there been such a circumstance then it would possibly be false, thus knowledge would be fallible, and I could no longer be said to know that I'm reading the paper now.

How is knowledge possible if it is possible that we err? That is the prime question of skepticism. Imagine, as the American philosopher Hilary Putnam did in 1983 in his book *Reason, Truth and History*, that a malicious scientist has taken the brain out of your skull, placed it in a vat of nutritious fluids, and rigged your brain with electrodes wired to a super-computer which stimulates your brain into believing that everything is normal, although it possibly couldn't get more abnormal. In this case you would not be able to know that you are not a brain in a vat because everything seems normal, and it is by the way false that you are reading the newspaper because this is something that the super-computer stimulates you into believing. Here is a possibility of error, and thus knowledge has been demonstrated impossible!

It is admittedly a relevant possibility of error that you have forgotten your glasses, and so you are not reading the newspaper but the *Yellow Pages*. But when the philosophers come to ask you whether it is a relevant possibility of error that you are a brain in a vat and so not reading the paper just seems ridiculous. Asking a physicist whether it is a relevant possibility of error that his voltmeter is calibrated incorrectly while attempting to measure the voltage drop over some circuit seems reasonable enough, to ask him about the brain in a vat story for a measurement error again seems stupid.

If we on the other hand accept the thought-experiment then we are left in the uncomfortable situation that none of us know whether we are brains in vats and thus just victims of the *Matrix* on a daily basis. The British zoologist Peter Brian Medawar (1915–1987) puts it very adequately:

> Medical scientists use the word 'iatrogenic' to refer to disabilities that are the consequence of medical treatment. We believe that some such word might be coined to refer to philosophical difficulties for which philosophers themselves are responsible.

Medawar as a zoologist is not the only one who has raised this complaint. Philosophers are and have been aware of this pitfall as the philosopher George Berkeley (1685–1763) prophetically puts it:

> Upon the whole, I am inclined to think that the far greater part, if not all, of those difficulties which have hitherto amused philosophers, and blocked up the way to knowledge, are entirely owing to ourselves. We have first raised a dust, and then complain that we cannot see.

Part of the story is, by the way, that Berkeley was a devoted idealist and thus thought that the only thing one could be really sure about was the existence of mind and that to exist is to be perceived by a mind. This is a troublesome stance; does a dust devil exist when it is not perceived? That's hard to see.

There are shelves and shelves worth of thought-experiments like the one cited above in contemporary philosophy and we are talking about some pretty bizarre philosophical beasts: Utility monsters and swamp men, devils and demons, ingenious mirror-installations and paper-mache barns, archers and Zen-masters – the list goes on *ad nauseam*. The book, *The Philosopher's Toolkit – A Compendium of Philosophical Concepts and Methods* (2001) which, as the title suggests is an introduction to the fundamental methods and distinctions in philosophy, reads accordingly regarding thought-experiments in science and philosophy:

6. Demonstrations

The difference between the thought experiments in science and philosophy, however, is that those in science often lead to physical experimentation. For philosophers, however, in most cases physical experimentation is unnecessary because what one is exploring is not the terrain of the physical but the conceptual universe. Reasoning out the leads of our imagination is often sufficient for concepts.

This sentiment does not seem entirely right. First of all, there are many thought-experiments in physics which are not amenable to physical experimentation. Second, there are still rules governing the use of thought-experiments in conceptual universes. The absurd world in which contradictions are true allows for all and nothing – *ex falso quidlibet*; from a contradiction everything follows which is easy to prove using a truth-table. For arbitrary statements A and B it is possible to demonstrate that a contingent statement follows from a contradiction

$$A \land \neg A \models B$$
$$\top \;\; \top \;\; \top \;\;\;\; \bot$$
$$3 \;\; 2 \;\; \uparrow \;\; 4 \;\;\;\; 1$$

and even worse, it is possible to show that something always true follows from something always false. As a tautology is true on empty premises there may as well be a contradiction on the left-hand side from which the tautology trivially follows:

$$A \land \neg A \models B \lor \neg B$$
$$\bot \;\; \bot \;\; \bot$$
$$2 \;\; 1 \;\; 3 \;\; \uparrow$$

Some have called upon such absurd constructions to salvage or undermine various theses. These situations are called 'impossible possible worlds'. Such situations are worse than the situation in which you are a brain in a vat because the latter are uncommon but at least logically possible, the former are just impossible! That something is physically impossible to carry out is acceptable, even in physics, when something is logically impossible, it is just impossible. If thought-experiments are not governed by at least what is logically possible, they are not ruled by anything other than your fantasy and imagination. And even if we restrict attention to what is logically possible it may just be that the justifying intuition is being outstripped by fantasia as the American philosophers Daniel Dennett and Douglas Hofstadter put it:

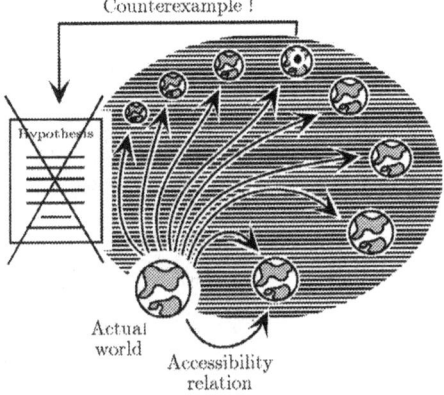

FIGURE 6.1. Relevant counterexample.

When philosophical fantasies become too outlandish – involving time machines, say, or duplicate universes or infinitely powerful deceiving demons – we may wisely decline to conclude anything from them. Our conviction that we understand the issues involved may be unreliable, an illusion produced by the vividness of the fantasy.

Epistemology, like much other philosophy, indulges in advancing theses and then attempts to find counterinstances to the theses making them go down in flames. This is may be a sound practice as a simple instance of refutation or falsification.

The counterexample must however be accessible or *relevant*— just like Gettier's. Relevance is dictated through accessibility criteria inherent in the particular model of inquiry. Once the counterexample hits in the range of relevant situations (also sometimes referred to as relevant 'possible worlds') in the model of inquiry that is usually the end of that thesis about knowledge (figure 6.1).

In some quarters of epistemology for instance the use of counterexamples is somewhat less regimented. Perceptual equivalents like identical twins or mirror-installations as counterexamples are allegedly more immediately accessible and relevant than brains in tanks of fluid. Whether identical twins on a far out heavenly body like Alpha Centauri are close enough to the actual situation to warrant relevance is more difficult to assess. It is not always obvious what counterexamples may be relevantly cited in disputes. If a claim to knowledge holds in the relevant situations, then a

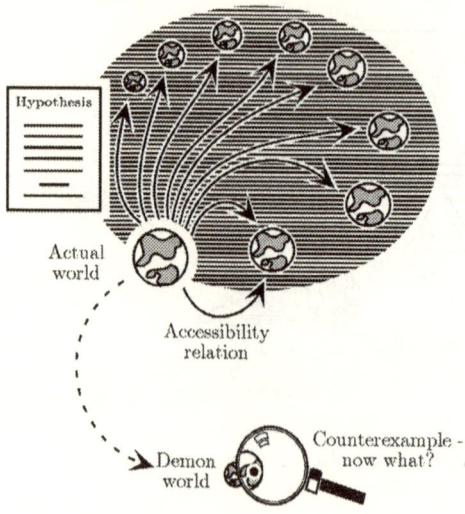

FIGURE 6.2. Irrelevant counterexample

counterexample on Alpha Centauri does not necessarily falsify the theses about knowledge entertained here in the actual situation (figure 6.2).

The more lack of structure, the more counterexamples come within the scope of relevance. It requires quite *some* intuition to go out to Alpha Centauri to set up a counterexample about infinitely deceiving demons either making the person in question believe that everything is normal when it is not, or systematically produce images to the person of pink elephants or flying toasters when there are none, etc. Suppose such a counterexample is constructed out there relative to some knowledge claim made in the actual situation.[1] The question is where the counterexample is to be assessed. On Alpha Centauri it holds so it makes little sense to assess it there. Thus, it must be assessed in the actual situation and the only way to do so is by consulting the intuitions over again. The intuitions present in way-off thought experiments or fictions serve a double purpose: First they are used as engines to cover the trip to Alpha Centauri, and then they may be used to justify that intuitively an error is committed here given a scenario

---

[1] If the knowledge claim is made on Alpha Centauri all bets may be off. There is no guarantee that the agent's cognitive apparatus works anything like the way it works in the actual world let alone that knowledge means anything like what it is taken to mean under normal circumstances.

6. Demonstrations

intuited there. In the worst case, it seems to be the case that using intuitions in this way becomes a self-fulfilling prophecy for counterexamples wherever leaving very little structure behind.

To consider whether a counterexample is relevant we need to know what it takes to get out there, and back, and, as opposed to a round-trip ticket, it cannot, without some structural argument, be the same thing. Chances are in these cases that the counterexample itself is underdetermined so the intuitions will be too.

Similar skeptical sentiments toward the use of intuitions have been expressed by other philosophers: 'If a view conflicts with intuition, then so much the worse for intuition' Laurence and Margolis summarize with respect to the American philosopher, Donald Davidson's, 'swampman' example:

> Swampman is a physical duplicate of a normal human being but happens to be created by a freak accident [out of a swamp]. Intuitively it seems that Swampman has beliefs and desires just as his duplicate does but this conflicts with various accounts of the nature of mental states, accounts that take an organism's history to be crucial to whether it can have contentful mental states. Daniel Dennett says the example is 'not worth discussing'. David Papineau, summarizing his own and Ruth Milikan's earlier responses to the example says that 'we both gave the same response to the intuition that such a being would, contrary to our theories, have contentful beliefs and desires. Namely, that since we were offering a posteriori theories of representation, rather than conceptual analyses of an everyday notion, we were prepared to reject the common-sense intuition that Swampman has contentful states.

There is another issue to consider when using examples to verify statements or hypotheses. *If thou look for verifications, thou shall find.* The Austrian philosopher of science Karl Popper (1902–1994) once scrutinized the psychologist Alfred Adler's (1870–1937) theory of 'individual psychology' in which all human motivation and behavior is governed by inferiority complexes. In the paper 'Science: Conjectures and Refutations' delivered before the British Council in the Summer of 1953, Popper concluded the following pertaining to Adler's theory:

> I may illustrate this by two very different examples of human behavior: that of a man who pushes a child into

the water with the intention of drowning it; and that of a man who sacrifices his life in an attempt to save the child. Each of these two cases can be explained with [...] ease [...] in Adlerian terms. [...] According to Adler the first man suffered from feelings of inferiority (producing perhaps the need to prove to himself that he dared to commit some crime), and so did the second man (whose need was to prove to himself that he dared to rescue the child). I could not think of any human behavior which could not be interpreted in terms of either theory. It was precisely this fact – that they always fitted, that they were always confirmed – which in the eyes of their admirers constituted the strongest argument in favour of these theories. It began to dawn on me that this apparent strength was in fact their weakness.

On this score the explanatory power of Adler's theory is not its advantage but *the* drawback. Verifications for the theory may be found even on examples of opposite nature. The theory is not much different from a tautology which is true on empty premises, hence always true but uninformative. This led Popper to certain conclusions about scientific theories which in turn also explains why informative talk uses contingent statements rather than tautologies:

1. It is easy to obtain confirmations, or verifications, for nearly every theory—if we look for confirmations.

2. Confirmations should count only if they are the result of risky predictions [...]

3. Every 'good' scientific theory is a prohibition: it forbids certain things to happen. [....]

4. A theory which is not refutable by any conceivable event is non-scientific. Irrefutability is not a virtue of theory (as people often think) but a vice.

6.3 Squaring the Opposition

When citing examples to verify or refute a certain thesis one should not only make sure that the example is accessible and thus relevant, but also that it hits the thesis in the right logical way.

A counterexample to

$$\text{All Iraqis are militant} \qquad (6.6)$$

is not that

$$\text{No Iraqis are militant} \qquad (6.7)$$

but rather that there is at least one Iraqi person who is not militant, or more generally that

$$\text{Some Iraqis are not militant.} \qquad (6.8)$$

Similarly, a counterexample to

$$\text{Some Iraqis are militant} \qquad (6.9)$$

is not that

$$\text{Some Iraqis are not militant} \qquad (6.10)$$

but rather that

$$\text{No Iraqis are militant.} \qquad (6.11)$$

It is a common mistake not to get the quantity and quality of the statements used for examples and counterexamples right. Already Aristotle distinguished between four types of statements in this regard:

(**A**) All S are P *Universal affirmative*

(**E**) No S are P *Universal negative*

(**I**) Some S are P *Particular affirmative*

(**O**) Some S are not P *Particular negative*

Universal and particular statements differ with respect to *quantity* while affirmation and denial differ with respect to *quality*. The four statement types (**A**), (**E**), (**I**) and (**O**) stands in the following relationships to each other on the Aristotelian conception of things:

- (**A**)-(**O**) and (**E**)-(**I**) are *contradictory* opposites as the one is true when the other is false and vice versa.

- (**A**)-(**E**) are *contrary* opposites since they cannot be true at the same time, but may be false at the same time.

- **(I)**-**(O)** are *sub-contrary* opposites since they cannot be false at the same time, but may be true at the same time.
- **(A)**-**(I)** and **(E)**-**(O)** are *subalternate,* as **(A)**-statements logically entail **(I)**-statements, and **(E)**-statements logically entail **(O)**-statements.

The logical relations between the four statements may be represented in what since the Middle Ages has been known as the *square of opposition* (figure 6.2).

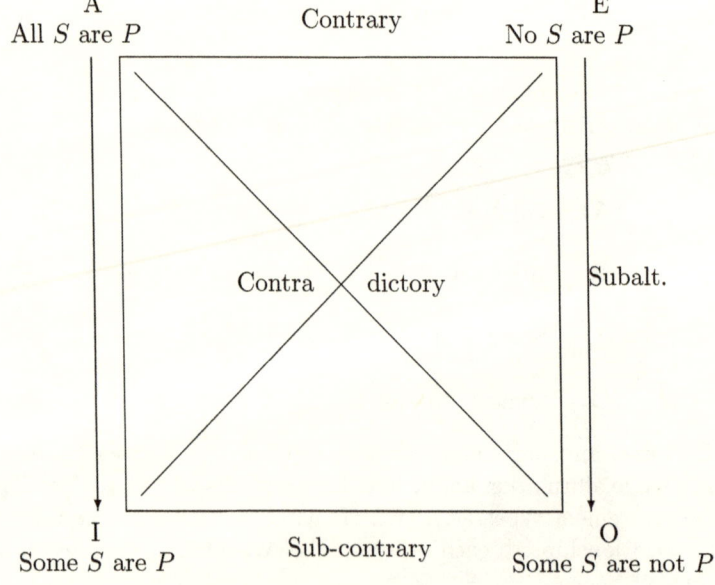

FIGURE 6.3. The Square of Opposition.

6. Demonstrations   75

The statement
$$\text{All Iraqis are militant} \qquad (6.12)$$
will normally entail, as Aristotelian subalternation would have it, that
$$\text{Some Iraqis are militant} \qquad (6.13)$$
but not vice versa. Just because some Iraqis may resort to guns does not entail that all Iraqis will so one cannot make a valid jump from (6.13) to (6.12). This is known as the problem of *induction*. When someone criticizes an opponent for generalizing or categorizing it is typically a criticism based on making an unwarranted and invalid inductive generalization going from something like (6.13) to something like (6.12). This fallacy has also been known since Antiquity. The skeptics, Carneades and Archilaus, took over Plato's Academy and paid homage to the well-known dictum that
$$\text{All I know is that I don't know} \qquad (6.14)$$
which sounds close to what Donald Rumsfeld said during the Defence Briefing. Later, another skeptic, Sextus Empiricus, charged Carneades and Archilaus for being dogmatic by showing that (6.14) rests on an unwarranted inductive generalization for its validity:

> It is also easy, I consider to set aside the method of induction. For, when (the dogmatists) they propose to establish the universal from the particulars by means of induction, they will effect this by a review either of all or of some of the particular instances. But if they review some, the induction will be insecure, since some of the particulars omitted in the induction may contravene the universal; while if they are to review all, they will be toiling at the impossible, since the particulars are infinite and indefinite. Thus, on both grounds, as I think, the consequence is that induction is invalidated.

This counter-argument against inductive inference is still in vogue today and used continuously. Whenever someone generalizes by saying 'All ...' the strategy for proving him wrong is to point out that not all possibilities are accounted for by the quantifier 'All' in the argument and there is thus a counterexample possible or real. If the counterexample is found, then the contradiction is immediate given the (**A**)-(**O**) of the square of opposition and the inductive argument goes down in flames. The difference between the aforementioned proof by induction and the current situation is that for the proof by induction one is licensed to take the next step given the previous one but that is not typically the case for enumerative inductive constructions used in everyday debates.

From a modern logical point of view the square of opposition is not entirely right as all the relations do not hold. For (**A**)-(**O**) and (**E**)-(**I**) statements the contradictory relationship stand. (**A**)-(**I**) statements are not subalternate from the modern point of view however because the domains of discourse are allowed to be empty—thus there might not be an object which has the property S, and so 'Some S are P' would be false even if the (**A**) statements is true. The same goes for (**E**)-(**O**) statements and the reason is the same. Furthermore, statements are only contrary and sub-contrary if the domain of discourse is not empty.

Assuming however that we are talking about something rather than nothing such that the domain of discourse is non-empty, then all the relations hold in the square of opposition. In everyday discourse it is mostly assumed that talk is about something and here the Aristotelian distinctions between contradictory, contrary and sub-contrary statements are very useful.

6.4 I Think I'm Talking

There is much more to be said for reasoning, logic and proper expression but enough is enough for a crash course. Whenever you deliberate and discuss from now on, make sure that

$$I \text{ think I'm talking} \qquad (6.15)$$

is true.

Further Reading

Thinking it Through, by Kwame Anthony Appiah. New York: Oxford University Press, 2003.

Language, Proof and Logic, by Jon Barwise and John Etchemendy. Stanford: Center for the Study of Language and Information; Package edition, 2002. Including the programs *Tarski's World 5.0* and *HyperProof*.

Asking the Right Questions: A Guide to Critical Thinking, by M. Neil Browne, Stuart M. Keeley. Prentice Hall, 2003.

How to Win Every Argument: An Introduction to Critical Thinking, by Nicholas Capaldi. MJF Books, 1999.

Logic, Language, and Meaning, Volume 1: Introduction to Logic, by L.T.F. Gamut. Chicago: University Of Chicago Press, 1990.

Modal Logics and Philosophy, by Rod Girle. McGill-Queen's University Press, 2001.

Thinking Things Through, by Clark Glymour. Cambridge: MIT Press, 1992.

Modern Elementary Logic, by Vincent F. Hendricks and Stig Andur Pedersen [in Danish / *Moderne elementær logik*]. Copenhagen: Høst and Soen, 2002.

Mainstream and Formal Epistemology, by Vincent F. Hendricks. New York: Cambridge University Press, 2006.

Critical Thinking and Communication: The Use of Reason in Argument, by Edward S. Inch, Barbara Warnick, and Danielle Endres. Allyn & Bacon, 2005.

The Experience of Philosophy, edited by Daniel Kolak and Raymond Martin. New York: Oxford University Press, 2006.

Logic: A Very Short Introduction, by Graham Priest. New York: Oxford University Press, 2001.

Argument, Critical Thinking, Logic and the Fallacies, by John Woods, Andrew Irvine and Douglas Walton. Prentice Hall, 2000.

The Stanford Encyclopedia of Philosophy, principal editor, Ed Zalta. Stanford: Stanford University, 2006.

About the Author

Vincent F. Hendricks holds two doctoral degrees (dr. phil and PhD) in philosophy and is Professor of Epistemology, Logic and Methodology and member of IIP, the Institut Internationale de Philosophie.

His work concentrates primarily on bringing mainstream and formal approaches to epistemology together—from epistemic reliabilism, counterfactual epistemology and contextualism to epistemic logic, formal learning theory and what is called 'modal operator epistemology.' Modal operator epistemology, developed first by Hendricks in *The Convergence of Scientific Knowledge* (Dordrecht: Springer, 2001), since developed further in a number of papers and books – see in particular *Mainstream and Formal Epistemology* (New York: Cambridge University Press, 2006) – is the cocktail obtained by mixing alethic, tense and epistemic logic with elements from formal learning theory in order to study the limiting validity of convergent knowledge.

Vincent F. Hendricks is editor-in-chief of the journal *Synthese*, and the associated book series *Synthese Library*, and chief-editor of *New Waves in Philosophy* book series. Hendricks is also the founder of ΦLOG – *The Network for Philosophical Logic and Its Applications* and chief editor of ΦNEWS – *The Newsletter for Philosophical Logic and Its Applications*

Other books by the author include:

Mainstream and Formal Epistemology (New York: Cambridge University Press, 2006)

Formal Philosophy, edited with John Symons (New York: Automatic Press / VIP, 2005)

Masses of Formal Philosophy, edited with John Symons (New York: Automatic Press / VIP, 2006)

Game Theory: 5 Questions edited with Pelle Guldborg Hansen (New York: Automatic Press / VIP, 2007)

Philosophy of Mathematics: 5 Questions, edited with Hannes Leitgeb (New York: Automatic Press / VIP, 2007)

The Convergence of Scientific Knowledge (Dordrect: Springer, 2001)

Feisty Fragments: For Philosophy (London: King's College Publications, 2004)

Logical Lyrics: From Philosophy to Poetics (London: King's College Publications, 2005)

500 CC: Computer Citations (London: King's College Publications, 2005)

Self-Reference, edited with Thomas Bolander and Stig Andur Pedersen (CSLI Publications, 2006)

8 Bridges Between Formal and Mainstream Epistemology, Philosophical Studies, March 2006 (Dordrect: Springer)

Ways of Worlds I, Studia Logica, April 2006 (Dordrect: Springer)

Ways of Worlds II, Studia Logica, November 2006 (Dordrect: Springer)

Interactions: Physics, Mathematics and Philosophy, between 1840-1930, edited with Jesper Lützen, Klaus Frovin Jørgensen (Dordrect: Springer, 2006)

New Waves in Epistemology, edited with Duncan Pritchard (Aldershot: Ashgate Publishing, 2006)

Proof Theory, edited with Klaus Frovin Jørgensen and Stig Andur Pedersen (Dordrect: Springer, 2001)

Probability Theory, edited with Klaus Frovin Jørgensen and Stig Andur Pedersen (Dordrect: Springer, 2002)

Knowledge Contributors, edited with Klaus Frovin Jørgensen and Stig Andur Pedersen (Dordrecht: Springer, 2003)

First-Order Logic Revisited, edited with Fabian Neuhaus, Stig Andur Pedersen, Uwe Scheffler, and Heinrich Wansing (Berlin: Logos Verlag, 2004)

The Way Through Science and Philosophy: Essays in Honor of Stig Andur Pedersen, edited with H.B. Andersen, F.V. Christiansen, and K.F. Jørgensen (London: College Publications, 2006)

Modern Elementary Logic, authored with Stig Andur Pedersen [in Danish / *Moderne elementær logik*] (Copenhagen: Høst and Søn, 2002)

Index

$A_1, \ldots, A_n$, 19
K, 19
$K_\alpha A$, 55
$K_\beta C$, 55
$\Diamond$, 50
$\bot$, 20
$\cap$, 17
$\checkmark$, 32
$\cup$, 17
$\equiv$, 22
$\leftrightarrow$, 14
$\neg$, 14
$\models$, 19
$\not\models$, 19
ϕ, 37
$\rightarrow$, 14
$\Box$, 50
$\subseteq$, 15
$\therefore$, 12
$\top$, 20
$\vee$, 14
$\veebar$, 21, 22
$\wedge$, 14
w, 51

accessibility, 51, 69
Adler, A., 71
Allen, W., 2
Alpha Centauri, 54, 69
Annie Hall, 2
antecedent, 21
Archilaus, 75
argument, 11
    conclusion, 12
    formalization, 25, 26
    knock-down, 4
    premise, 12
    schema, 11
    soundness, 13
    Toulmin's model, 48
    validity, 12, 14, 19
Argument Clinic, 11
Aristotle, 2, 73
Asimov, I., 8
attitude, propositional, 55
awareness, 55

Beecher, L., 1
belief, 54, 62
Berkeley, G., 67
'bottom', 20
brain in vat, 66
Brown, R.M., 52
Bundchen, G., 53
Bush Jr., G.W., 49, 53

Carneades, 75
certainty, 55
ceteris paribus clause, 54
Christensen, H., 53
circularity, 47
classical logic, 49
Clinton, H.R., 45
conceptual analysis, 65
    'stretching', 66
condition
    necessary, 1, 22, 23
    sufficient, 1, 22, 23
connector word, 12, 13
consequent, 21
consistency, 2

data, 48
Davidson, D., 71
de Carvalho, C., 41
De Niro, R., 5
Deer Hunter, 5
definition, 1
    definiendum, 1
    definiens, 1
demonstration, 59
Dennett, D., 68
Department of Defence News Briefing, 3
Dole, B., 5
Dole, E., 45

Einstein, A., 56
Elvis fans, 46
epistemology, 62
ex falso quidlibet, 68
example, 62
    bad, 65
    counter-, 69
    good, 63
    relevance, 69
    verification, 72
explanatory power, 72

fallacy, 41
    Ad Baculum, 43
    Ad Hominem, 44
    Ad Ignorantiam, 47
    Ad Populum, 46
    Ad Verecundiam, 46
    affirming the consequent, 42
    denying the antecedent, 42
    petito principii, 47
falsity, 1
fantasia, 68
FBI, 58
feeling, 57
Figueroa, W., 4

Flynt, L., 58
formalization, 26
Forrest Gump, 40

genitalia, 54
Gettier, E., 63
Gore, A., 45
Greek alphabet, v

Hanks, T., 40
Heat, 5
Hofstadter, D., 68
Human League, 6
Hustler Magazine, 58

idealism, 67
inconsistency, 2
"individual psychology", 71
induction, 75
inferiority complex, 71
intension, 49
Internet, 5
intuition, 66, 70

Jackson, F., 66
jump, 41
justification, 62

Kant, I., 62
knowledge, 54, 62
    infallibility, 66
    standard definition, 62
    theory of, 62

language
    natural, 1, 49
    propositional, 14
Laurence, S., 71
Lewis, C.I., 62
Liar Paradox, 9
logical
    symbols, vi
logical connective, 14
    bi-implication, 14

conjunction, 14
disjunction (exclusive), 21
disjunction (inclusive), 14, 64
main, 19
material implication, 14
negation, 14
scope, 19
tableaux rules, 32
truth-functional behavior, 20
logical form, 3, 24

Marcos, F., 7
Marcos, I., 6, 50
Margolis, E., 71
Matrix, 54
McCarthy Senate Hearings, 44
meaning, 3, 6, 29
Medawar, P.B., 67
Milikan, R., 71
modality, 49
  alethic, 51
  deontic, 52
  epistemic, 52
  temporal, 52
Modus (Ponendo) Ponens, 16
Modus (Tollendo) Tollens, 15
Modus Ponendo Tollens, 17
Modus Tollendo Ponens, 17
Monty Python, 11
Moore, G.E., 4
Moore-paradox, 4
Moynihan, D., 58
Muhammad-drawings, 13

NAFTA, 45
necessity, 50
NRA, 53
NYSE, 9

operators, 50

opinion, 58

Pacino, A., 5
Papineau, D., 71
performative contradiction, 4
Perot, R., 45
personal pronoun, 58
Peter, L.J., 27
plant, 2
Plato, 62
Plato's Academy, 75
Popper, K., 71
possibility, 50
possible worlds, 69
Powell, C., 7
principle
  of bivalence, 1
  of compositionality, 20
  of extensionality, 49
  of non-contradiction, 2
proof, 15, 59
  by contradiction, 59
  by induction, 61
  direct, 60
  Reductio ad Absurdum, 60
proposition, 1
Putnam, H., 66

Quayle, D., 4

Rand, A., 43
Rumsfeld, D., 3
Russell, B., 63

semantic tableaux, 33, 35, 37
  counterexample set, 37
  heuristics, 39
semantical consequence, 19
semantics, 19
  extensional, 49
  intensional, 49
Sex and the City, 3

Sextus Empiricus, 75
situation, 3
    actual, w, 51
    closeness, 54
    other, v, 51
    proximity, 54
    similarity, 54
skepticism, 66
Smullyan, R., 10
square of opposition, 74
statement, 48
    (**A**), 73
    (**E**), 73
    (**I**), 73
    (**O**), 73
    analytic *a priori*, 6
    atomic, 18
    complex, 18
    contingent, 6, 24
    contradictory, 3, 24, 73
    contrary, 73
    counterfactual, 9, 52
    declarative, 1, 9
    deontic, 9
    formalization, 26
    interrogative, 9
    logical form, 14
    non-assortoric, 1
    presumptive, 9
    quality, 73
    quantity, 73
    self-referential, 9
    sub-contrary, 74
    subalternation, 74
    synthetic *a posteriori*, 7
    tautology, 5, 24
    well-formed, 18
Sting, 12
swampman, 71
syntax, 18

tautology, *see* statement
'top', 20

Toulmin, S., 48
transitivity, 60
tree, 32
truth, 1, 6, 51, 62, 63
truth-condition, 20, 51
truth-table, 20, 27
    'short', 30

UN Security Council, 7
underdetermination, 51
understanding, 55

validity, 19

Wachowski-brothers, 66
warrant, 48
wish, 57

X, Malcolm, 11

www.ingramcontent.com/pod-product-compliance
Lightning Source LLC
Chambersburg PA
CBHW021020090426
42738CB00007B/841